"Covenant theology—an essential dimension of Reformed theology—unites the sixty-six books of the Bible in beautiful, Christocentric harmony. Exploring the covenants of redemption, works, and grace, Ryan McGraw ably sketches the covenant motif from the seed promise in Genesis to the new Jerusalem in the book of Revelation. He demonstrates that grasping covenant theology helps us grow in our understanding of Scripture, our communion with the triune God that produces joy and piety, and our lives as individuals, families, and churches—all to the glory of the one who designed the marvelous plan of salvation. Covenant theology, then, is so magnificent because it is simply gospel theology that inevitably produces Trinitarian doxology."

**Joel R. Beeke,** Chancellor and Professor of Homiletics and Systematic Theology, Puritan Reformed Theological Seminary

"Ryan McGraw skillfully highlights the basics and blessings of covenant theology that first blessed him as he saw unifying themes in Scripture that helped him make sense of the parts. Writing with clarity and conviction, he introduces readers to the unity of the Bible, the triune God, and their implications for Christian living so that they will know God and his people in deeper ways. If you're looking for a doctrinally sound primer on covenant theology, this is a good place to start."

**Sarah Ivill,** author, *The Covenantal Life: Appreciating the Beauty of Theology and Community*

"The Protestant Reformer Martin Bucer, who was such a formative influence on John Calvin, maintained that 'True theology is not theoretical, it is practical; the end of it is to live a godly life.' Ryan McGraw's *What Is Covenant Theology?* exemplifies Bucer's conviction. Here is theology that is accessible, practical, and pastoral. McGraw has provided Christians with a theological primer that will enrich their lives and stir their hearts and minds to bow down and worship. This is a must read for Christians who desire to grow in the grace and knowledge of God."

**Ian Hamilton,** President, Westminster Presbyterian Theological Seminary, United Kingdom

T0284198

"Ryan McGraw has given the church a clear, concise, and accessible survey of one of the most important teachings in Scripture—the covenants that God makes with human beings. The argument of *What Is Covenant Theology?* is exegetically informed, theologically nuanced, and practically oriented. Whether familiar or unfamiliar with covenant theology, readers will profit from the way that McGraw helps us see the unity of the Bible and the glory of the covenant-making, covenant-keeping God of the Bible."

**Guy Prentiss Waters,** James M. Baird Jr. Professor of New Testament and Academic Dean, Reformed Theological Seminary, Jackson

"Ryan McGraw has written an excellent introduction to covenant theology—one that, as a pastor, I can hand to anyone in my church who wishes to know more about the covenant concept. While the book has a certain systematic approach, one will also encounter a rich biblical and Trinitarian theology permeating the chapters. I'd like to have written a book like this myself, but there is no need now with this fine contribution to Christian living. And make no mistake, the key to Christian living is understanding God's covenants."

**Mark Jones,** Senior Minister, Faith Presbyterian Church, Vancouver, Canada

"Ryan McGraw's introduction to covenant theology is wonderful. He takes a complex topic and boils it down to its basics, showing both covenant theology's distinctive emphases and how those distinctives are a blessing to God's people. I am confident this will invite many to study covenant theology more deeply and thus understand the Bible more completely."

**Stephen G. Myers,** Professor of Systematic and Biblical Theology, Puritan Reformed Theological Seminary; author, *God to Us: Covenant Theology in Scripture*

*What Is Covenant Theology?*

# What Is Covenant Theology?

*Tracing God's Promises through the Son,*
*the Seed, and the Sacraments*

Ryan M. McGraw

WHEATON, ILLINOIS

Trade paperback ISBN: 978-1-4335-9277-5
ePub ISBN: 978-1-4335-9279-9
PDF ISBN: 978-1-4335-9278-2

---

**Library of Congress Cataloging-in-Publication Data**

Names: McGraw, Ryan M., author.
Title: What is covenant theology? : tracing God's promises through the Son, the seed, and the sacraments / Ryan M. McGraw.
Description: Wheaton, Illinois : Crossway, [2024] | Includes bibliographical references and indexes.
Identifiers: LCCN 2023030931 (print) | LCCN 2023030932 (ebook) | ISBN 9781433592775 (trade paperback) | ISBN 9781433592782 (pdf) | ISBN 9781433592799 (epub)
Subjects: LCSH: Covenant theology.
Classification: LCC BT155 .M34 2024 (print) | LCC BT155 (ebook) | DDC 231.7/6—dc23/eng/20231207
LC record available at https://lccn.loc.gov/2023030931
LC ebook record available at https://lccn.loc.gov/2023030932

---

Crossway is a publishing ministry of Good News Publishers.

| BP | | | 33 | 32 | 31 | 30 | 29 | 28 | 27 | 26 | 25 | 24 |
|----|----|----|----|----|----|----|----|----|----|----|----|----|
| 15 | 14 | 13 | 12 | 11 | 10 | 9 | 8 | 7 | 6 | 5 | 4 | 3 | 2 | 1 |

*To Jonathan L. Master,*
*through whom God showed me covenant faithfulness by*
*being a friend and not merely a "boss" when I needed him*
*most in one of the most difficult seasons of my life*

# Contents

# Acknowledgments

IN TERMS OF DIRECT INFLUENCE, most of the people who made this book possible are long dead, and I acknowledge them in the footnotes. My wife, Krista, and children (especially Owen and Calvin) greatly helped move this material forward into book form by expressing their enthusiasm for it, both at conferences and in family worship.

The entire team at Crossway has been an over-the-top outstanding, professional, and all-around impressive group of people. Samuel James and Kevin Emmert deserve special gratitude. Samuel took a chance on an author less familiar to Crossway's readership because he believed in the merit of the project. He showed tremendous patience when my first attempts were mediocre, generously offering more time and feedback than I have ever seen to a stranger with no contract in place. As for Kevin, I could not imagine a more competent and skilled editor, who sympathized with and understood my intent, often intuitively, taking what I was trying to say and helped me say it clearer and better. Pairing an opinionated author and editor together could go sideways pretty quickly. Kevin was always gracious, respectful, and even excited about the book, and I think I almost always gave in to his suggestions without contest.

I dedicate this book to Jonathan Master: You have seen me at my worst and did everything in your power to bring me back to my best. The Lord showed covenant faithfulness to me, while suffering from a failing body and mind, through your kindness, patience, friendship, generosity, and forward thinking. Thank you for helping me rest after a great series of trials and for making teaching and living richer in Christ.

I trust that the Son is pleased in what glorifies the Father in these pages, and that the Spirit with shining the spotlight on the Son. May the Spirit magnify Christ in every reader's heart, even as he did in mine while writing, that together we might thank and love our Father in heaven.

Introduction

# Why Do the Basics and the Blessings Go Together?

KNOWING THE BASICS of covenant theology brings great blessings with it. In fact, this book will show that the main blessings of covenant theology lie in its basic principles. Yet it is easy for the average reader to get lost in large tomes on the subject. Serving as a key for reading the entire Bible, "introductions" to covenant theology swell into many pages quickly. This small book aims to introduce readers to the basics of covenant theology in light of the blessings that covenant theology brings. Highlighting some of these blessings shows how covenant theology can strengthen our walk with God, making the path before us a bit smoother and easier. The basics and blessings of covenant theology are inevitably very personal as well.

## A Personal Journey

Growing up in a non-Christian home, I knew nothing about the Bible. I did not know who the apostle Paul was until I started reading the New Testament, around the time the Spirit brought me to Christ at age sixteen or seventeen. The church I attended was dispensational, which taught that God had different plans for the Jews and for the church, resulting in a disjointed reading of the Old and New Testaments.[1] Implicitly, I learned that Christians did not need to keep the Ten Commandments. Theoretically, I was "antinomian," which describes someone who believes that those justified by Christ do not need to keep God's law. However, the Holy Spirit often trains our hearts before straightening out our heads. Thus, reading Jesus's application of the Ten Commandments in the Sermon on the Mount, I found myself praying, "Lord, make me like this!" even though I thought at the time that he was altering or removing the Old Testament law. Covenant theology was the blessing that I did not know I needed in order to read the Bible better and to live well for God's glory. Gradually, I saw the Son (Jesus), his seed (offspring) in the church, and the sacraments (let's say *signs* for now) as unifying themes in Scripture that helped me understand the parts.

Covenant theology came to me in two ways. First, the church I attended inculcated two vital practices: Christians read their Bibles every day, and Christians tell others about Jesus. Consistent Bible reading worked something profound in many people in that church. In my case, Jesus's teaching in the Sermon on the Mount started to sound a lot like what I was reading in Exodus and Leviticus. People began raising questions about God's election, human free will, the depths of human sin, the Spirit's work in people's hearts, and, ultimately, how the Old and New Testaments fit together. Second, since this church could not answer most of these questions, people found resources like Ligonier Ministries, which led me to works like the

---

1 For a useful critique of this view, see Keith A. Mathison, *Dispensationalism: Rightly Dividing the People of God?* (Phillipsburg, NJ: P&R, 1995).

Westminster Confession of Faith, Calvin's *Institutes*, and Charles Hodge's *Systematic Theology*.[2] Suddenly, I and others began finding answers. Whether such issues related to the unity of the Bible, to the work of the triune God in saving sinners, or to Christian living, covenant theology seemed to answer key questions. Jesus, who saved one church in both Old and New Testament, was the focal point of the Bible, and baptism and the Lord's Supper drove these truths home vividly.

While covenant theology bears almost innumerable blessings, the breathtaking unity of Scripture, the glory of the triune God, and its implications for the Christian life stand out as central ones. In this introduction, I explain each of these areas briefly in a somewhat natural and disjointed way to introduce the plan for the rest of the book. These three blessings lead us to reflect on the basics of covenant theology as they revolve around Jesus Christ, as they affect his church, and as they come home to us in word and sacrament.

## What Blessings of Covenant Theology Stand Out?

Covenant theology is a "big picture" issue, describing the relationship between God and his people throughout the ages. It is not merely about some parts of the Bible or specific theological and practical questions. It shows us how to see the unity of the Bible's message, how to read the whole Bible, how to know God, and how to live. When embraced, it deepens our communion (or fellowship) with the triune God and with others in the church. How, then, is covenant theology a blessing?

2  Westminster Assembly, *The Confession of Faith, and the Larger and Shorter Catechism: Agreed Upon by the Divines Assembled at Westminster* (London, 1655); John Calvin, *Institutes of the Christian Religion*, ed. John T. McNeill, trans. Ford Lewis Battles (Philadelphia: Westminster, 1960); Charles Hodge, *Systematic Theology*, 3 vols. (1871; repr., Grand Rapids, MI: Eerdmans, 1999).

First, covenant theology is a blessing because it shows the breath-taking unity of Scripture. From the first promise of the Seed of the woman who would crush the serpent's head (Gen. 3:15) to one of the last promises of God's heavenly dwelling with his people as their God (Rev. 21:3), covenant theology pulls together everything in between. The result is that we view the Bible more like a grand epic narrative than a collection of short stories. God's promise to undo the ruin that Satan brought through sin is like a seamless thread that ties together all the pages of Scripture. In this light, the promise to Abraham that in his Seed all the nations of the earth would be blessed (Gen. 22:18) fits both Genesis 3:15 and Galatians 3:14, in which "the blessing of Abraham" applies to believers now. The Seed of the woman's suffering in the place of his people resurfaces in important passages like Psalm 22, Isaiah 53, and Romans 16:20. Moses's leading the people out of Egypt, and everything else he did, flowed from God's remembering his covenant with Abraham, Isaac, and Jacob (Ex. 2:24–25). David looked to God to forgive sins and change hearts (Ps. 51), and he pleaded that the Deliverer would come through one of his descendants (2 Sam. 7; Pss. 89; 132). Solomon celebrated God's faithfulness in establishing his Seed (of the woman) over the ends of the earth, bringing blessings to all nations (Ps. 72). Peter urged believers to look to Christ's return, teaching them that God preserves the world now for the sake of the elect, just as he did in Noah's covenant in Genesis 6–9 (2 Pet. 3:8–9). Covenant theology is a blessing because all of Scripture, no matter what book we find ourselves in, reminds us of other parts. The entire book is about God's covenant with his people, always pointing them to Christ (Luke 24:44–46). Not only does the Old Testament fit with the New but the New starts to look like an inevitable result of the Old, without which the story would be incomplete.

The breathtaking unity of Scripture should fill us with awe and wonder. Many people ask how the Bible can be God's word when men wrote it. How can we expect any kind of unified message from men, who wrote parts of the Bible in different centuries, resulting in alleged contradictions? Yet seeing the theme of God's covenant, which he placed clearly throughout Scripture, shows that allegations of contradictory messages by many authors stem largely from ignorance of what the Bible actually teaches. My favorite example was reading Isaiah 53, about the suffering "servant," to a Muslim while I was in college. He rejected the idea that Christ was God and that he suffered in the place of sinners. Yet when I read the text to him, he thought I was reading from the New Testament, only to be surprised that Isaiah seemed to describe Christ's sufferings more vividly, in some respects, than Matthew and Paul. God's word is breathtaking. Whatever difficulties we perceive at first in particular parts of Scripture start resolving themselves when we understand how the parts fit into the whole. Christ is the central theme of God's relationship to his church, in both Testaments. Sacraments like circumcision, the Passover, baptism, and the Lord's Supper simply illustrate the point and drive it home. God's consistency in the Bible is both spiritually breathtaking and invigorating.

Second, covenant theology is a blessing because it highlights the glory of the triune God. This point may take a while for many of us to appreciate. Whether or not we realize it, we come to the Father, through the Son, by the Spirit (Eph. 2:18). Salvation is about the glory of the triune God, and covenant theology is the vehicle through which God reveals himself and his saving message. The Father saves us, through the Son, by the Spirit (Eph. 1:3–14) so that by the Spirit, through the Son, we come to the Father. Paul summarized the gospel in terms of God's sending his Son to become man, whom the Spirit vindicated, so that we might believe in him (1 Tim. 3:16). We often undercapitalize on the vital importance of the Trinity in Christian faith and life because no one has taught us what to look for in the Bible. Yet covenant theology is like painting a verbal picture of God; the one God of Israel shows us over time that he is Father, Son, and Spirit, inviting us into intimate fellowship with himself.

How does covenant theology relate to the Trinity? The simple answer is that God's story, which he tells through covenant relationships, is ultimately about himself. The gospel is about God, and the more fully we grasp the gospel, the more clearly we see God. An illustration can show how easily we lose sight of this fact. What often happens when someone asks a believer to give their "testimony"? Is it not common to hear people talk about what a mess their lives were before Jesus came along? They were drug addicts, homeless, in prison, suffered from depression, and so on, and now they could not make it a day without Jesus. Yet if we ask them who Jesus is, maybe they cannot say much about his divine identity; his two natures; his office as prophet, priest, and king; or his humiliation and exaltation. Testimonies can quickly become more about us than about the God who saves us, devolving into stories that are not too different from people trusting a "higher power" through groups like Alcoholics Anonymous. Yet Paul did not testify to himself; he testified to Christ Jesus as Lord (2 Cor. 4:5). Covenants are first and foremost about God. The Old Testament primarily tells us what God is like through his names, attributes, and works, with a gradually increasing focus on the work of the Father, the Son, and the Spirit in saving us. Teaching us who God is more fully, it was virtually impossible for the New Testament writers to explain the promises of the new covenant without Trinitarian terms. Our baptism (which is a covenant sign) is one of the greatest proofs of the fact (Matt. 28:19). Baptism places God's "name" on us, telling us that God must be our Father, that Jesus must be our Savior, and that the Spirit must dwell in our hearts. The sacraments direct us to the Son so that we might be God's seed. Covenants testify to the triune God, leading us to echo the Bible in glorifying the triune God.

Third, covenant theology is a blessing because it helps us learn to live the Christian life. We will see that covenants include parties, conditions, promises, and sanctions (or consequences for unbelief and disobedience). Thinking about walking with God in every part of life, we should want to trust, love, and obey him. Covenants teach how to do so in light of our relationship with God (parties), what God wants us to do in that relationship (conditions), how to live by faith in Christ (promises), and how to keep moving toward heaven (sanctions). When you read the Ten Commandments that God gave Israel, for example, the most important questions to ask are, What kind of relationship did these people have with God, and what kind of relationship do I have with God? God redeemed or saved them from Egypt by his grace, and God graciously redeems me from my sin in Christ. The God who saved them commanded them to obey him because they loved him, and so he does with me. If the relationship is basically the same in both cases, then loving the law of the Lord becomes a great means of loving the Lord of the law (Ps. 119 throughout).

Covenants clearly teach us how to live with other Christians in the church. The church is the Son's seed, which he plants, waters, and nourishes through word and sacrament. God covenants with groups of people and not merely with individuals. Baptism and the

Lord's Supper, as signs pointing us to what God's promises mean, remind us that we not only hope in Christ but are in the Christian life together for the long haul. And are we not thankful that we do not have to live the Christian life alone? Covenant theology teaches us to live the Christian life in the right context, and to love the church of Christ as we increasingly love the Christ of the church. Covenant theology leads us by the hand to think about Christian living, both for individuals, families, and churches. It teaches us the practical uses of the sacraments and the importance of public, family, and private worship, bringing God's blessings to every area of life. Christ is the Son, who is the hero of the story; we are his seed, or children, living together in his church; and the sacraments point to our relationship with the Son and his seed at the same time.

## What Is the Plan for the Rest of This Book?

The rest of this book explains more fully why covenant theology is a blessing in relation to the Bible, the Trinity, and the Christian life. These blessings (unity, Trinity, and Christianity) turn out to be the basics of what we need to know about covenant theology as well, with the Son (covenant Savior), the seed (covenant church), and the sacraments (covenant signs) appearing regularly at key points in the story. While this book cannot answer every question about covenant theology, it aims to show you why this teaching is a God-given blessing to believers. Due to how much ground it covers, I have devoted three chapters to the breathtaking unity of Scripture, one to the Trinity, and one to the Christian life. Each of these chapters includes study questions that promote reflection and good conversation with others about what the Bible teaches. The final chapter answers questions related to common issues that arise when studying covenant theology, and the recommended reading resources provided in the back of the book help readers go further and dig deeper.

The bottom line is that covenant theology helps us read well, praise well, and live well. As you read this book, pray that the Spirit would enable you to see the unity of Scripture, to love the glory of God, and to live the Christian life.

## Questions

1. Summarize what you currently know about covenant theology. What unanswered questions do you have?

2. Why is studying covenant theology worthwhile?

3. How can seeing a unifying theme in Scripture be helpful as you read through the Bible?

4. How can covenant theology help you pursue a deeper relationship with God?

5. What is your view of the role of the church in the Christian life? How important is the church in your walk with God?

1

# Covenant Theology and
# the Unity of Scripture

HAVE YOU EVER STRUGGLED to understand what is in the Bible? God could have said anything that he wanted to, so why do we have so many laws about sacrifices in Leviticus? Why are there ten chapters of genealogy starting 1 Chronicles? How do we piece together the picture of God appearing in fire and darkness on Mount Sinai with the account of Jesus coming as the light of the world? How can reading the Bible help me live life day to day when I just don't see how so many of its details are relevant to, say, caring for my children today or going to work or school? Finding unifying themes in the Bible, especially as they relate to who God is, who we are, what our problem is, and what God has done about it may not give us what we are looking for as we read Scripture, but they direct us instead to what we need. We need a God who shows us his Son, our Savior, as we live our lives as part of his church. As we will see below, God made his Son the centerpiece of the biblical message.

Covenant theology helps us see the breathtaking unity of Scripture, making all the parts begin to fall into place over time. The best thing is that the more often we read the entire Bible, with covenant theology in hand, the better the parts will start explaining each other. We can see this fact by asking what a covenant is, how covenants unify the theme of the Bible, what the divisions of the covenant of grace are, and how covenants help us read the Bible with spiritual joy in Christ.

## What Is a Covenant?

In order for a definition to be helpful, it needs to be broad enough to pull in everything to which it applies, and it needs to be narrow enough to distinguish concepts from each other. If we define a triangle as a shape, then our definition is too broad because squares and circles are shapes too. Yet defining triangles as isosceles is too narrow because not every triangle has two sides that are the same length. However, defining a triangle as a polygon with three edges and three vertices shows that a triangle is a specific shape.

The same rule applies to defining *covenants*. If we define covenants too broadly as mere relationships, then we cannot distinguish covenant relationships, for example, from my relationship with my neighbor's dog. Defining covenants too narrowly, however, as "a bond in blood sovereignly administered" rules out some biblical applications of the term covenant, as with marriage, David's covenant with his friend Jonathan, and many others.[1]

For these reasons, older Reformed authors defined covenants, more or less, as agreements or contracts that bind two or more parties together by promises, conditions, and sanctions.[2] While every definition

---

1 O. Palmer Robertson, *The Christ of the Covenants* (Phillipsburg, NJ: Presbyterian and Reformed Publishing, 1980), 4.

2 One of my favorite examples of how this broad definition includes all kinds of covenants is Patrick Gillespie, *The Ark of the Testament Opened, or, The Secret of*

of *covenant* is likely imperfect to some extent, this one at least takes into account every use of the many uses of the word in Scripture, especially in the Old Testament. For example, David and Jonathan were parties in the covenant between them. Jonathan promised loyalty to David, and David promised to preserve Jonathan's family when he became king. God bore witness, implying judgment (sanction) against either side if one of them broke the conditions of the covenant (1 Sam. 20). The two men already had a relationship as friends, but now they were bound in covenant through an oath, establishing a special kind of relationship with special obligations.

God's covenants with his people are contracts or agreements as well. Revolving around promises through God's oaths (which make promises in God's name and with God as witness), covenants include demands, whether repentance[3] toward God and faith in Jesus Christ (Acts 20:21) or living blameless (sincere) lives before God (Gen. 17:1), sanctioning those rejecting God's terms. Calling God's covenants "contracts" or "agreements" is not demeaning to God because he does not have to bind himself to anyone in a special covenant relationship.[4] He is God, and we must believe and obey him, whether or not he

---

the Lords Covenant Unsealed: In a Treatise of the Covenant of Grace, Wherein an Essay Is Made for the Promoving [sic] and Increase of Knowledge in the Mysterie of the Gospel-Covenant Which Hath Been Hid from Ages and Generations but Now Is Made Manifest to the Saints (London: R.C., 1661).

3 Repentance means turning from sin, turning to God in Christ, and turning to new godly practices in the place of those sins. Jesus is the pivot on which repentance turns since it is only in Christ that we find forgiveness for our sins and the ability to turn from sin as he gives us the Holy Spirit to help us.

4 See Westminster Confession of Faith 7.1 (hereafter cited as WCF): "The distance between God and the creature is so great, that although reasonable creatures do owe obedience unto him as their Creator, yet they could never have any fruition of him as their blessedness and reward, but by some voluntary condescension on God's part, which he hath been pleased to express by way of covenant." In *Creeds,*

promises to give us anything in return (Luke 17:10). Unlike human beings, God is free to make covenants with us, but we are not free to refuse them once he makes them. Lots of examples would strengthen this definition of covenant, and its advantages are that it has stood the test of time, that it is easy to understand and remember, and that it reflects every use of "covenant" in the Bible.

## How Do Covenants Unify the Themes of the Bible?

Sometimes the best way to make sense of what we find in the Bible is to step back and look at the big picture. As Fred Sanders remarks, we see the triune God best by rereading the Bible in light of the whole.[5] Once we see the end of the story, then we can better appreciate all the parts that led to the end. We understand the Bible better generally when we reread it repeatedly. The sacrifices in Leviticus and genealogies in Chronicles tell us more about what God is like and what he is doing after we read Hebrews and Matthew, for example. On a broader level, the Bible tells us ultimately that the Bible's story begins before the Bible. The story of God's covenants flows from eternity to eternity, through what people have called the covenants of redemption, works, and grace. While some of the parts of this story will not be as obvious as others initially, they become clearer as we see how these three covenants (one in eternity and two in history) pull in the entire narrative. In each of these three cases, the Bible does not use the term *covenant* right away. Though this can appear to give us a false start, the next chapter illustrates why the rest of the

---

*Confessions, and Catechisms: A Reader's Edition*, ed. Chad Van Dixhoorn (Wheaton, IL: Crossway, 2022), 195 (hereafter cited as *CCC*).

5   Fred Sanders, *Fountain of Salvation: Trinity and Soteriology* (Grand Rapids, MI: Eerdmans, 2021), 199.

Bible's story does not make sense without these covenants holding the rest of the parts together.

Beginning at the end of the Bible can help us get started. Describing the "holy city, new Jerusalem" (Rev. 21:2), coming down from heaven, Revelation 21:3 says, "And I heard a loud voice from the throne saying, 'Behold, the dwelling place of God is with man. He will dwell with them, and they will be his people, and God himself will be with them as their God.'" All God's covenants with his people promised eternal life in his presence, making him our God and us his people, requiring faith and obedience, and threatening judgment against apostasy[6] and disobedience. At the end of the story, we see that God has always been, and always will be, true to his word. He is our God, we are his people, and he dwells among us. Through faith in God's promises, with repentance and obedience to his commands, we escape the wrath to come and enjoy everlasting life, which is knowing him (John 17:3). We should always look forward to this final installment of God's covenant as we read our Bibles, live the Christian life, and use every Lord's Day (Sunday) to look to the final day of the Lord. God's unified covenant story in Scripture leads from eternity to eternity. Doing so helps us appreciate the main "stages" of the plan in the covenants of redemption, works, and grace. God planned to be with us, we left him, and he brings us back to himself in Christ through the Spirit.

### The Covenant of Redemption

We assume a lot when we tell people about the gospel. Knowing who God is, we know who we are, what our problem is with God, and what God has done to save us. Yet people who don't know what

---

6　Apostasy is the act of falling away from or rejecting profession of faith in Christ.

God is like don't really know who they are, what their problem is, or even the fact that they need salvation. Regardless of where we start in talking to unbelievers, our challenge is to bring them up to speed in all these areas. Yet sometimes Christians need to be brought up to speed too. If we finish our Bibles and pay attention well, then we realize that something important came *before* the foundation of the world in Genesis 1:1. The *covenant of redemption* tells us what that is.

The covenant of redemption is the first stage of the unified message of Scripture. This covenant is between the persons of the Trinity in eternity. Redemption means "the act or process of buying back," and in this context it refers to God's covenant to send Christ to do what needed to be done to purchase our salvation and buy us back from the consequences of our sin. We don't pick up the covenant of redemption from the first pages of the Bible, but, like the Trinity, it becomes clear when we reread the book. The parties in the covenant of redemption are the Father and the Son with the consent of the Spirit. The Father promised the Son, on the condition of his incarnation, to give him the nations as his inheritance (Ps. 2:8), to exalt him with the name above every name (Phil. 2:9–11), to give him the Spirit to pour out on the church (Acts 2:33), and many other things that Christ alone can claim. The Son became man, negatively, to take up the conditions of becoming a curse for his sinful people, who broke God's law. Positively, the Son as man came to do God's will (Ps. 40:8) and to fulfill "all righteousness" for his sinful people or seed (Matt. 3:15; cf. Heb. 2:13). The covenant of redemption includes us, but only as the objects of the Son's work and as part of his reward. This is why some have called this covenant "the covenant of the Mediator."[7] It is more about

---

7   Reformed authors have given the covenant of redemption various names like the covenant of suretyship, the covenant of the mediator, and the counsel of peace. *Sure-*

COVENANT THEOLOGY AND THE UNITY OF SCRIPTURE

the Savior than it is about the saved. The Father designated the Son to save his seed, to whom he would later speak in word and sacraments.

We are not parties in the covenant of redemption, which is unconditional respecting God's elect people. It is eternal, and it shows the single will of the triune God exercised from the Father, through the Son, by the Spirit. The relations among the persons of the Trinity are eternal and unchangeable, not covenantal. God does not agree to become triune. Rather, he does what he does because he is who he is. Yet the covenant of redemption shows how the single will of God is exercised from the Father, through the Son, by the Spirit for our salvation. Rather than God having three wills, this is more like the divine will in origin, in action, and in perfection. This covenant is distinct from any covenants God made in history because the Father promised things to the Son that no one else can claim, because the Son fulfilled conditions and bore sanctions that no one else could bear, and because Christ "purchased" and sends the Spirit in a way that no one but God can send. The covenant of redemption is not the covenant of grace, which is a historical story rather than an eternal plan, but the covenant of redemption is the foundation of the covenant of grace.[8] Just as we cannot build a good house without a solid foundation, so we cannot build a covenant theology without a stable foundation in the triune God. God's plan to save his seed, though his Son, is the foundation for calling them by word and Spirit and sealing them with sacraments.

---

*tyship* means that Christ is our surety, standing in our place before God. *Mediator* means roughly the same thing, Jesus mediating between God as the offended party and us as the offending party. *Counsel* refers to the intra-Trinitarian covenant, and *peace* refers to the result of Christ being surety and mediator between us and God.

8  For more about the covenant of redemption, see J. V. Fesko, *The Trinity and the Covenant of Redemption* (Fearn, UK: Christian Focus, 2016).

## The Covenant of Works

Moving from the heights of eternity to the depths of the earth, God's first covenant in history is often called the *covenant of works*. This refers to God's covenant with Adam and Eve, from whom everyone else came. People have called it a covenant of *works* not because the first couple's obedience was somehow worthy of reward from God but because he promised them life if they kept trusting him and obeying him. The book of Genesis, where this covenant appears, sets the stage for the Bible's story, leaving room to fill in the details more clearly as the story unfolds.

Like most things in Genesis, God did not reveal the covenant of works in explicit words, but he drops us into a narrative filled with covenant ideas. The parties of the covenant of works were God and Adam. The tree of life embodied its promise (Gen. 2:9), symbolizing eternal life in God's presence (see Rev. 22:2–3, where the end of the story helps us understand the beginning again!). Perfect obedience was the condition of the covenant, to which the tree of the knowledge of good and evil pointed (Gen. 2:9). Though this tree looked like the others in the garden of Eden (Gen. 3:6), what made it special was that God said not to eat its fruit. What greater test could God give Adam and Eve of whole-soul committed obedience to himself, since the command rested on nothing more than God's authority? Just as young children sometimes need to obey their parents because they love and trust them, even if they don't understand their commands, so we must always trust and obey God simply because he is God. Death was the sanction of the covenant, warning that Adam would surely die if he ate from the wrong tree (Gen. 2:17). Though God did not use the word *covenant* in Genesis 2 or 3, what more details could we need to find a covenant here? Adam and Eve did not deserve everlasting life for their obedience because they owed obedience to their Creator regardless. Sometimes people have called this covenant a "covenant of life"[9] due to its implied promise. Most have called it a covenant of works with respect to its condition. Either way, the covenant of works went beyond Adam and Eve's general relationship to God as their Creator. They should have trusted and obeyed God because he is God; by covenant, God promised them a reward for doing so.

The covenant of works did not end well. Barely two chapters into the Bible, everything goes sideways. When Adam and Eve sinned by eating the forbidden fruit, they "died." Again, Genesis shows this in an understated, implicit, and gradual way. The first couple likely did not understand what death meant, since it was not a part of human experience in the garden, yet death came in many forms. God cast them away from the tree of life, barring the way back with a well-armed angel (Gen. 3:24). The world became less hospitable to human life, and Adam's labor over the ground as well as Eve's labor in bearing children brought pains with them. Their first son murdered their second (Gen. 4:1–16), and the list of their descendants bore the chilling refrain "and he died" (Gen. 5). Showing that Adam's sin did not affect his heart and life alone, generations of his children mimicked his sin and built on it until "every intention of the thoughts of [man's] heart was only evil continually" (Gen. 6:5). God then wiped out the world through a universal flood, showing that sin brought his wrath and curse. Is this not a realistic description of the world we live in now? Do we not see a collapsed world under a broken covenant of works in hard jobs, painful childbirth, illness and death, broken families, war, natural

9   Westminster Shorter Catechism (hereafter cited as WSC) q. 12 (*CCC* 413).

CHAPTER 1

disaster, and a host of opinions about religion? The covenant of works can help us show nonbelievers that the Bible accurately describes and explains the world as it really is.

Man's environment, relationships, and course of life were tainted with the death of sin, and man's heart was dead toward God—and so remains (Eph. 2:1). The natural climax to this litany of death in the early chapters of Genesis was the death of the world through a universal flood. While the flood waters washed away almost all sinful humanity from the world, this dreadful judgment did not wash away the filth of man's heart (Gen. 8:21). And so the world continues. Death begins in the heart, and our bodies and environment bear symptoms that all is not right with the world because people are not right with God.

To make sure we are clear at this point, how did mankind "die" in the garden? We died spiritually, losing upright hearts, being cast out of God's life-giving presence. We die physically; the life spans of Adam's children even gradually decreased. We continue to die daily, through the sufferings of this life, even in common tasks like work and childbearing. And, unless God does something to save us, we will die universally (and eternally), just like the world died in the flood. Putting things more theologically, without Christ we are dead in Adam because we sinned in Adam (Rom. 5:12). Human beings are in trouble because they bear "the guilt of Adam's first sin, the want of original righteousness" (which was part of Adam's nature at creation), and the corruption of their whole natures, which the church has "commonly called original sin."[10] Original sin does not mean the first sin committed by human beings, but it describes the origins of sin in every one

10  WSC q. 18 (*CCC* 414).

of us because of what Adam did. This point will come back even more clearly as we continue to listen to God's covenant story below. When we see and feel the miseries of sin, when we hate our jobs, struggle through childbirth, fear "natural" disasters, are repulsed by war and death, and attend funerals, then we should see a broken covenant of works as the culprit.

Some people object to the idea of a covenant of works because the term does not appear in Genesis 2–3. Yet without the covenant of works, we cannot adequately understand the covenant of grace in Christ, which we need so desperately. Looking at the whole Bible, we should realize that we are "overhearing" a conversation between God and Adam about a covenant in Genesis 2–3. A friend of mine illustrates this fact by asking how we would interpret an overheard phone conversation if we heard someone using terms like "bride," "groom," "bridesmaids," "best man," and "invitations." How could we not conclude that they were talking about a wedding? Likewise, when we overhear all of the parts of a covenant in Genesis 2 (parties, promises, conditions, and sanctions), we should understand what God is talking about, even if the word *covenant* is not there.[11]

Something even more powerful and important helps us along, however. At the first Lord's Supper, which is a sacrament or covenant sign of God's promises, Christ called his finished work on the cross "the new covenant in my blood" (Luke 22:20). What Christ did fulfilled a covenant, and we enter this covenant when we receive Christ. Yet just like the Bible's story in the Old Testament becomes clearer as we keep reading, so later parts of the New Testament clarify and explain

---

11  This illustration comes from J. V. Fesko in a conference talk at the Greenville Presbyterian Theological Seminary Spring Theology Conference, "The Covenant of Redemption," March 2021.

earlier ones. In Romans 5:12–21, Paul explains both Genesis 2–3 and what Jesus did in the Gospels by drawing important parallels between our relation to Christ and our relationship to Adam. Through Adam's unrighteous act, many became sinners. Through Christ's righteous act on the cross, and through his righteous life, many were made righteous (Rom. 5:19). This gives us two sides of an equation. On the one hand, when Adam sinned, God counted (or imputed) his sin to his people. On the other hand, when Christ obeyed, God counted (or imputed) his righteousness to his people. Adam and Jesus have a unique relationship to people that no other human beings have. Both acted in the place of their people, and their actions brought consequences, whether bleak or glorious, on the entire group. This is why Paul added elsewhere that just as all who are in Adam die, so all who are in Christ are made alive (1 Cor. 15:22). If our relationship to Christ as our representative is by covenant, then how can our representation in Adam not be? The sacrament of the Lord's Supper shows our covenant relation to the Son as his redeemed seed, who saves us from being Adam's lost seed.

While no one can earn eternal life again through the covenant of works, we cannot fully grasp the way to life in Christ without it. In the covenant of redemption, the Father planned to send the Son to "save his people from their sins" (Matt. 1:21), with the Spirit's help and blessing (Isa. 11:1–6; John 3:34). As our prophet, priest, and king, Christ bore the sanctions of the broken covenant of works through his sufferings, and he fulfilled its conditions in our place through his obedience. Though the Bible says far less about the covenant of works than it does the covenant of grace—to which we turn next—we must keep the covenant of works in mind so that we can understand the problems that the covenant of grace solves.

## The Covenant of Grace

Our friendships say a lot about who we are. For example, the righteous should choose their friends carefully, knowing that the ways of the wicked lead them astray (Prov. 12:26). Friendships can make or break people, shaping who we are and making us better or worse for the experience. We tend to become like our friends, and our friends become like us. The covenant of grace is about making enemies with sin and Satan, and restoring friendship with God and his people, making us ultimately like Christ, who laid down his life for his friends (John 15:13).

Most of the Bible is about the covenant of grace, and the covenant of grace is about Christ (the Son). Westminster Larger Catechism 31 says, "The covenant of grace was made with Christ as the second Adam, and in him with all the elect as his seed."[12] We need a better representative than Adam; we need new hearts, and we need to be like God. Put differently, we need Jesus to be our Savior, the Spirit to dwell in our hearts, and God to be our Father. Genesis 3:15 through Revelation 22 is a single story about how God does this great work. Genesis 3:15 gives us the basic ideas of the covenant of grace, serving as a gateway into the rest of the Bible, making it a key to seeing the breathtaking unity of Scripture. This may be both the most basic and most blessed verse on covenant theology in the Bible.

To understand Genesis 3:15, we need to get oriented to who's who. The text says,

> I will put enmity between you and the woman,
>     and between your offspring and her offspring;

---

12  Westminster Larger Catechism (hereafter cited as WLC) q. 31 (*CCC* 345).

he shall bruise your head,
    and you shall bruise his heel.

There are three contrasts in this text: the woman and the serpent, the Seed and the serpent, and the Seed and the seed.[13] "Offspring" in the ESV and "seed" in my translation mean the same thing here. First, beginning where the problem started, Eve fell into sin by making friendship with the serpent and eating the forbidden fruit. God would put an end to this alliance by putting "enmity" between the serpent and her, breaking her friendship with sin and Satan. "Enmity," like the word "enemy," means the opposite of friendship. By sinning, Eve acted in enmity toward God, treating Satan as her friend, but God would break this relationship. Second, skipping to the end for a moment, the serpent would crush the Seed's heel, while the Seed would crush the serpent's head. Translating the idea here can be tricky, but "bruise" is a bit weak. "Crush" ups the stakes a bit more appropriately. The Seed is singular, and he singularly suffers and undoes the curse of sin that the serpent brought on human-ity. Since the serpent would crush the Seed's heel but have his head crushed, the serpent gets the harsher outcome of the encounter. Third, in the middle of the verse the seed is also plural, pitting Satan's (or the serpent's) people against the woman's people. This sets the pattern for the division of nations in Genesis, pitting the seed of the woman against the seed of the serpent. Just as the church is associated with Christ, so the world is associated with Satan. This is where the notorious ten chapters of genealogy in 1 Chronicles becomes relevant. Chronicles, and other places in the Bible, mark off the serpent's seed from the woman's seed, which marks the division between the world and the church. Though

---

13  See John White, *A Commentary upon the Three First Chapters of the First Book of Moses Called Genesis* (London: John Streater, 1656), on Gen. 3:15.

sacraments come later in the story, they will point to the Son saving the seed, following the outline established in this verse.

So how does Genesis 3:15 put the covenant of grace in a nutshell? When God saves sinners, he ends our alliance with sin and Satan, like he did with Eve. He does so by sending the Seed, the Christ, to destroy death (1 Cor. 15:54), Satan (Heb. 2:14), and the works of the devil (1 John 3:8). Yet the Seed represents a seed (Ps. 22:30). What Christ did, he did for and in the place of his people, affecting the whole group, which we call the church. Christ saves his people from their sins (Matt. 1:21), keeping them in the world while they are not of the world (John 17:15). It takes the rest of the Bible to show how Genesis 3:15 is a unifying thread running through the whole.

A few examples have to suffice here, promoting clear eyesight to see the breathtaking unity of Scripture rather than commenting on the entire Bible. First, Hebrews 2:14 says that Christ died "that through death he might destroy the one who has the power of death, that is, the devil." Destroying the devil explains what crushing the serpent's head means in Genesis 3:15. Drawing parallels to lots of other related verses shows what this entails. Satan was the "strong man" who bound people in the misery of sin. Now Christ has bound him, plundering his goods (Matt. 12:29). The false "ruler of this world," Satan, is "cast out" (John 12:31) through Christ's death on the cross. Though Satan walks about like "a roaring lion" seeking to devour people (1 Pet. 5:8), he is a defeated enemy who has "great wrath" because "he knows that his time is short" (Rev. 12:12). When the Seed of the woman crushed the serpent's head, Satan's relationship to the world changed. Though he remains active, he is not alive and well. Jesus destroyed, bound, crushed, and cast him out. As we know by experience, as well as from Scripture, he is not bound or destroyed in a way in which he does nothing. We often wish this were the case! Yet Christ bound him "that he might not deceive the nations any longer" (Rev. 20:3). While we might struggle with such bold statements, we should never underestimate how far and wide the Spirit has spread the gospel to this day, beginning in the book of Acts. Satan is like a fatally wounded warrior, who knows that he is already dead, yet who hates his enemies so much that he continues to claw after them until his dying breath. Both the spread of the church and its suffering through history exemplify these facts. A worldwide church is a clear indicator that the Seed of the woman has crushed the serpent's head, which should encourage us to pray and persevere in a world that is hostile to Christ and his gospel.

Second, Paul told the church in Rome that "the God of peace will soon crush Satan under your feet" (Rom. 16:20). This statement takes Christ's victory over Satan from the end of Genesis 3:15 and combines it with the separation of the woman's seed and the serpent's seed in the middle. Christ gained victory over sin, death, and Satan for his people, and his people share in his victory over Satan. Through sin, Satan was our "father," and when we sinned we did his will instead of God's (John 8:44). Friendship with the world, the flesh, and the devil is enmity with God (James 4:4). Now that Christ is on our side and has made us his friends, our victory over Satan is sure. What greater encouragement could we have in our personal battles against sin and through the church's fears of wars, rumors of wars, opposition, and persecution?

Third, both the Seed and the seed tie together the covenant of grace nicely in Galatians 3. Without getting into every detail, the fact that Paul has God's covenant dealings with Abraham and Moses as well as Genesis 3:15 in view makes this example powerful for pulling large sections of the Bible together. In Galatians 3:16, Paul writes, "Now to Abraham and his Seed were the promises made. He does not say,

'And to seeds,' as of many, but as of one, 'And to your Seed,' who is Christ" (NKJV).[14] Jesus Christ is the Seed of the woman who would crush the serpent's head. Yet later in 3:29, Paul adds, "And if you *are* Christ's, then you are Abraham's seed" (NKJV). This "seed" is the church, which stands against Satan's seed in the world. Appealing to a sacrament, or covenant sign, Paul brings God's covenant promises home by saying, "As many of you as were baptized into Christ have put on Christ" (3:27), making Jews and Gentiles, slaves and freemen, men and women "all one in Christ" (3:28). The Son saves his seed, sealing them in a sacrament, because the Seed of the woman crushed the serpent's head. Paul explains in this chapter God's intent in the Mosaic law by appealing to God's covenant with Abraham, which clearly uses the terms of and applies the promise of Genesis 3:15.

Ideas like this should encourage us because what is true of Christ becomes true of his people. God would as soon reject the Son's seed as he would reject his Son. Our friendship with God is just as secure as Jesus's place with God. Genesis 3:15 showcases the breathtaking unity of Scripture in ways that few other verses (if any) can. God makes friends with us, through his Son, and by his Spirit. Jesus's work results in crushing our enemy, forgiving our sins, changing our allegiances, and making us like God again. Because the Seed of the woman saved his seed by crushing the serpent's head, we have a friend who changes both where we stand with God and what we are like in our lives.

## Conclusion

How do we see the breathtaking unity of Scripture through covenants so far? Though we have not yet looked directly at texts where the term

14 While the ESV translation "offspring" is correct, the NKJV, which is equally correct, stresses the "seed" parallel I am making here.

*covenant* appears (and they are many!), the covenants of redemption, works, and grace give us a map to lead us through the whole Bible. In the covenant of redemption, the triune God planned to save elect sinners, and Christ agreed to stand in their place. The covenant of works shows how and why they need to be saved, and the covenant of grace shows how they come to receive Christ for salvation. Christ is the hero of the covenant of grace, and most of the Bible tells the story, either of what he would be and do or who he is and what he has done. The goal of the covenant of grace is to make those who were God's enemies through the covenant of works his friends in Christ, who fulfilled the covenant of redemption.

So, do you struggle with what is in the Bible? Maybe the solution lies in learning what to look for. Ultimately, we cannot read the Scriptures to learn how to be better wives, husbands, parents, children, employees, and friends if we lose sight of who God is, who we are, what our true problem is, and what God has done about it. This is precisely where covenant theology gives us what we need, pulling our relation to God into all other areas of life and directing us to see Christ through every book of Scripture. We look next at the "divisions," or stages, of the covenant of grace.

## Questions

1. What should a good definition do? Give some examples of defining something too broadly or too narrowly.

2. Which definitions of *covenant* take in all kinds of covenants in the Bible? What alternative definitions have you heard, and what are their advantages and disadvantages?

3. In your own words, what are the covenants of redemption, works, and grace? Who are the parties in each? What are their promises, conditions, and sanctions?

4. Why is the covenant of works still relevant to us today since we cannot gain God's favor through our obedience?

5. Describe some ways in which Genesis 3:15 is so helpful in understanding and applying the whole Bible. How can this text help you explain the Bible's story in your Bible reading and family worship?

2

# The Covenant of Grace

DIVERSE PEOPLE can still share unity. I attended high school in Huntington Beach, California, and many of my friends were American, Peruvian, Polish, Japanese, Mexican, English, and German. We looked, and sometimes spoke, differently from one another, and we had overlapping stories that brought us all to Huntington Beach High School. Friendship unified this diverse group of people as well, building on and creating common interests without erasing differences.

God's covenant history is similar. One covenant theme ties together parts and people from vastly different contexts, backgrounds, and cultures. God's single story of the covenant of grace took centuries to tell. In fact, it is not a stretch to say that everything from Genesis 3:16 to Revelation 22:21 is a detailed exposition of Genesis 3:15. Like a unifying theme in a symphony, the Son, the seed, and the sacraments pervade the diverse moments and movements in the Bible's story, often revolving around God's work in the lives of important people. These include primarily Adam, Noah, Abraham, Moses, David, and Christ. While these moments constitute one gradually expanding covenant of grace, we can divide them into the old and new covenants as well. The old covenant takes in the first five stages, from the beginning of the world to the coming of Christ, while the new covenant envelops only the last, from Christ's finished work to his second coming.

Using the Son, the seed, and the sacraments as guideposts, we will first trace the stages of the covenant of grace in biblical history in this chapter and then address the division of our Bibles into the old and new covenants and the Old and New Testaments in the next. Getting the basics of the storyline correct here opens new vistas of blessings to us as we prayerfully read our Bibles.[1]

## Adam to Christ: Introduction

I teach future ministers in a theological school. I also administer ordination exams to such men in my church. One of the things that these men need to be able to do is identify the primary stages of the covenant of grace in the Bible. What we are really asking them is, Can you show me the unified theme of Scripture so that you can fit any part of the Bible you are teaching or preaching into the storyline? The answer we expect from them is something like this: Adam (Gen. 3:15), Noah (Gen. 6–9), Abraham (Gen. 12; 15; 17; 22), Moses (Ex. 20–24), David (2 Sam. 7; Ps. 89), and Christ (Matt. 26:28). Using these stages and texts as guideposts shows the blessed and breathtaking unity of one covenant of grace. It leads us through the pages of Scripture from beginning to end, and the Son, the seed, and the sacraments teach us what to look for.

1  I preached a series of seven sermons on covenant theology following the themes of the Son, the seed, and the sacraments at Cliffwood Presbyterian Church (PCA) in Augusta, Georgia, in November 2021, which can be found online at Ryan R. McGraw, 2021 Christian Life Conference series, SermonAudio.com, October 15–17, 2021, https://www.sermonaudio.com/solo/cliffwoodpres/sermons/series/153654/.

## Adam to Noah

We have already seen God's promise to Adam in Genesis 3:15, with some key places where its teaching reappears in the Bible. Noah marks the next stage in the story in Genesis 6–9. Bringing judgment on the world for its sinful rebellion, the Lord saved the seed of the woman in Noah's family because he would one day send the Seed to undo the ruin and misery of sin. God preserved the covenant of grace in Noah's family: even though the godly line of the church continued with Shem, and Ham's family fell into the seed of the serpent, Japheth was given hope that one day he would "dwell in the tents of Shem" and thus share in Shem's blessings (Gen. 9:27). Though this may appear a bit obscure, it was an early way of saying that the nations would eventually come under the covenant of grace. Shem was God's seed, and the nations descending from Japheth would eventually come under Shem's covenant tent. Knowing that God revealed himself and his promises gradually but consistently helps us tuck away details like these for later.

Sacraments are signs that point to the central promises of God's covenants. They are also seals, which means that they confirm his promises to his people. Like a government seal on a driver's license, sacraments show that God's covenant promises are authentic and that they belong to us. The tree of life served this role in the covenant of works, and the rainbow did so in the Noahic covenant (Gen. 9:13). The rainbow was a sign that God would keep the world from another flood, to preserve the seed of the woman, until he sent the Seed of the woman to save them from sin. Though we can't touch, taste, or smell it, it is a seal by which God authenticated his promises to remember his grace to the world for the sake of his church.

Noah's covenant was the covenant of grace with "common grace" benefits to the world, delaying final judgment until God calls his elect to himself. Grace means giving good things to those who don't deserve them. Common is opposed to special. Put together, God's people are the focal point of the Noahic covenant, bringing undeserved good things to everyone else. At least the apostle Peter seemed to think this way. Looking to Christ's second coming, he reminded his readers that people forgot God's judgment and grace under the Noahic covenant (2 Pet. 3:1–6). He added that the covenant of grace still brings common grace benefits to the world as we wait for Christ's return, because God is "patient toward you, not wishing that any should perish, but that all should reach repentance" (2 Pet. 3:9). The Noahic covenant teaches us that God tolerates a lost and dying world because his kindness, forbearance, and patience calls people to repentance while there is still time (Rom. 2:4). God is still calling his people by his word and Spirit, which is the only reason why the world is still here. Every meal we eat, every time the leaves change in the fall and the flowers come out in spring, and every wedding we celebrate should remind us that God preserves the world for the sake of the covenant of grace. Do we respond well to God's common grace (before it is too late) by reaching out for his special grace in Christ?

### Abraham

Next in history comes Abraham, whose name dominates much of the rest of the Bible. We saw this in Galatians 3 already: if we want salvation in Christ today, then we need to have the "blessing of Abraham" (Gal. 3:14). Before he became Abraham ("father of many"), God called and separated Abram ("father") and his seed from the nations, promising him land as a pledge that God would be their God, they would be his people, and he would dwell among them (Gen. 12, 15). God took up the responsibility for fulfilling this covenant by passing between the parts of Abram's sacrifice while Abram was sleeping (Gen. 15). Since the time that Adam broke the covenant of works, sacrifices always served as sacraments of the covenant of grace, signifying that the Seed of the woman would save his seed through shedding blood, giving his life for their lives. Sacrifices were Old Testament sacraments in that they, as signs, pointed to God's promised salvation. Though believers laid hold of those promises through sacrifices, they trusted in the promises rather than in the sacrifices. Back to Abram, as God confirmed the covenant while he slept, so our hope for salvation must rest on God's action rather than ours.

God expanded his promises to Abram, calling him to faith and obedience (Gen. 17:1), promising to be his God and the God of his seed after him. He also changed Abram's name to Abraham because his covenant blessings would overflow to the nations (Gen. 17:5; 22:18). Circumcision was the primary sacrament of this covenant, pointing to the Son's work in saving sinners through faith (Rom. 4:11). Circumcision pointed both to Christ's work in taking away his people's sins (Col. 2:11–12) and to the Spirit's work in changing their hearts (Deut. 10:16; 30:6). This is likely why Jesus expressed surprise that Nicodemus, a prominent Jewish teacher, did not know that one needed to be "born again" to enter the kingdom of God (John 3:3, 7). We cannot have friendship with God unless the Spirit creates enmity with sin and Satan through a change of heart.

The promises of the covenant of grace under Abraham belonged to believers and their children, even though not every child in the covenant was of the covenant. In other words, not every child who inherited Abraham's promises shared Abraham's faith in the coming

Christ. Paul taught good Old Testament theology when he argued that a true Jew is not one who is a Jew only outwardly and that true circumcision was not merely outward in the flesh, but true circumcision is in the heart, thus making one a true Jew (Rom. 2:28–29). Even though God ordained sacraments to drive people to the Savior, sacraments have always made poor saviors. Yet people have always fallen into hoping in the sacraments themselves, especially circumcision and baptism, rather than in the God of the sacraments. Most pastors likely know how often people ask for baptism for their children, even when they don't believe in Christ or go to church, thinking that baptism will make them safe. I have often been surprised how regularly such phone calls come to churches I have pastored. How different this is from what God taught Abraham through circumcision, and how similar it is to unbelieving Israelites, who were circumcised in flesh but not in heart! Sacramental signs of God's covenant promises teach adults and children receiving them to live by those promises. God also invited household male servants and foreigners to receive Abraham's covenant promises and to join the seed of the woman by being circumcised (Ex. 12:44, 48).

The Abrahamic covenant teaches us that the Seed of the woman would bless and save all the nations of the earth, calling them to repent and be circumcised, promising to be the God of believers and their children, as well as of strangers in their midst. God still calls us and our families to Christ, using the terms of Abraham's covenant. We should believe because the promise comes to us. We should hope in God for our children because the promise still belongs to them too. And we should pray for the spread of the gospel because God is calling many from afar to be Abraham's seed (Acts 2:38–39). One reason why most Christians in history have historically baptized households (including infants) is that Peter applied God's promises to Abraham's household to anyone in the world who comes to Christ.

## Moses

Coming next, the Mosaic covenant also dominates the pages of the Old Testament. Due to factors like how law is emphasized in this covenant, how the book of Hebrews contrasts it to the new covenant, and how much of the Mosaic covenant can sound like the broken covenant of works, this covenant has proved harder to understand and more controversial than the other stages of the covenant of grace.[2] Older authors liked to call the Mosaic covenant the "legal administration" of the covenant of grace because law and threats stand out, though alongside gracious promises.[3] Yet this should not lead us to lose sight of its central promises, which greatly expanded the blessings of the covenant of grace.

At least two texts stand out, placing the Mosaic covenant squarely in the covenant of grace. First, Exodus 2:24 introduces the entire narrative, in which Moses is a key figure, by stating that "God remembered his covenant with Abraham, with Isaac, and with Jacob."

2  I address a few of these issues in the question-and-answer section that closes this book.

3  E.g., John Ball, *A Treatise of the Covenant of Grace Wherein the Graduall Breakings Out of Gospel Grace from Adam to Christ Are Clearly Discovered, the Differences Betwixt the Old and New Testament Are Laid Open, Divers Errours of Arminians and Others Are Confuted, the Nature of Uprightnesse, and the Way of Christ in Bringing the Soul into Communion with Himself, Are Solidly Handled* (London, 1645), 100–101; Patrick Gillespie, *The Ark of the Testament Opened, or, the Secret of the Lords Covenant Unsealed: In a Treatise of the Covenant of Grace, Wherein an Essay Is Made for the Promoving* [sic] *and Increase of Knowledge in the Mysterie of the Gospel-Covenant Which Hath Been Hid from Ages and Generations but Now Is Made Manifest to the Saints* (London: R.C., 1661), 155.

Why did God raise up Moses as a prophet, priest, and ruler over his people? Because he was still preserving his seed (the church) until the Seed of the woman (the Son) should save his people as their prophet, priest, and king. As the Lord preserved Christ's seed under Noah and expanded his promises to them under Abraham, so Exodus through Deuteronomy builds on the covenant with Abraham, exemplifying, expounding, and expanding its blessings.

This reminds us that every stage of the covenant expands on the last. Moses taught the need for circumcised hearts explicitly, while Abraham knew it only implicitly. The narrative assumes at the outset that we are tracking with the covenant of grace from Adam, through Noah, to Abraham, expecting more detail under Moses. The Mosaic covenant is a blessing to us because we see more of God, more of his law, and more of his promises than we do under Adam, Noah, and Abraham.

Second, Exodus 20:2 lays the Mosaic covenant on a gracious foundation, introducing the Ten Commandments by saying, "I am the LORD your God, who brought you out of the land of Egypt, out of the house of slavery." "The statutes and the rules" in the Ten Commandments, which summarize the covenant God made with Moses (Deut. 5:1–5), distinguished the seed of the woman from the seed of the serpent while attracting some of the nations to God (Deut. 4:6–8). Does this not remind you of Abraham? Wisely summarizing the "preface" to the Ten Commandments, Westminster Shorter Catechism 44 notes, "The preface to the Ten Commandments teacheth us, that because God is the Lord, and our God, and Redeemer, therefore we are bound to keep all his commandments."[4] What more could we want to identify

---

4  WSC q. 44 (*CCC* 420). Among many more examples, Neh. 9 and Pss. 106–107 are good examples of looking back to redemption from Egypt as calls to faith and repentance for later generations.

the Mosaic covenant with the covenant of grace, looking to Christ as Redeemer and the Seed of the woman? Under Moses, God called his people to faith, repentance, and obedience. God still promised to be their God and the God of their seed after them. God redeemed them from slavery in Egypt because he would save his people from their sins in Christ. God anticipated Joshua's conquest of Canaan, which was a symbol that he would be their God, that they would be his people, and that he would dwell among them.

While giving attention to the intense emphasis on law under the Mosaic covenant, we can neglect the virtual explosion of sacraments, signifying and sealing God's gracious promises. Not only circumcision but also the Passover, the sacrifices, the priesthood, and even the tabernacle—in which God would show his covenant presence—were signs and seals of the covenant of grace under Moses. All these expanded and explained in more detail what Christ would do. Most pointedly, the tabernacle as the centerpiece of Mosaic worship highlighted the centerpiece of the covenant of grace: God is our God, we are his people, and he dwells among us. The whole book of Leviticus showed God's covenant people that there was a way back to him from sin, giving people hope of dwelling in his presence.[5]

Without sidelining the gracious character of the Mosaic covenant, it is worth clearing the ground a bit lest we stumble over some details. Though the "legal" aspects of this covenant are not equivalent to the covenant of works, they relate to that covenant in at least two key ways.

First, the threats of the law told anyone receiving the covenant signs that without faith in the coming Seed of the woman, they remained

5  For a superb study of such themes in Leviticus, see L. Michael Morales, *Who Shall Ascend the Mountain of the Lord? A Biblical Theology of the Book of Leviticus*, New Studies in Biblical Theology 37 (Downers Grove, IL: IVP Academic, 2015).

dead in their sins. Even though the main purpose of the law here is to show believers how to believe, repent, and live in the context of God's gracious covenant, bad news always looms in the background for those refusing to listen (e.g., Lev. 26; Deut. 28). God used the same law in the covenant of works and the Mosaic covenant, though for different purposes in different contexts. Yet how can anyone rejecting God's promises and spurning his commands expect anything less than death in Adam instead of life in Christ? While most of us don't like being rebuked or corrected, we must realize that God designed covenant threats to bless us by driving us to Christ. Would it really be grace to let you ruin a marriage through internet pornography or destroy relationships through lying and begrudging forgiveness? How much more does God's law graciously promote a right relationship with God? We never lose anything by confessing sin and coming to Christ. Those who cover their sins will never prosper, but God's covenant mercies always come to those who confess and forsake them (Prov. 28:13). The Mosaic covenant stressed a gracious use of the law, which the covenant of works could not achieve on its own.[6]

Second, the Mosaic covenant illustrates how Christ would fulfill the covenant of works, according to the terms of the covenant of redemption. Christ obeyed the covenant of works for his people, keeping God's commandments and living by them (Lev. 18:5; Rom. 5:12–21). He also bore the curse of the broken covenant, becoming a curse for us on the cross (Deut. 21:23; Gal. 3:13). He did this as a better prophet,

---

6  Reformed theologians have called this the "first use of the law," which is the first of three uses. The gospel alone creates the first use of the law because the covenant of works can bring conviction, but it says nothing about Christ. The second use of the law is restraining outward evil in society, while the third, and primary, use of the law is a rule of life for believers who want to imitate God's character.

priest, and king than Moses, who could not ultimately save anyone because he could neither die for their sins nor change their hearts. The sacraments of the Mosaic covenant were defective by design, with an expiration date, teaching people to look for something better and more permanent in Christ. Bloody sacrifices were repeated daily and yearly, priests had to cleanse themselves and eventually they died, and the ark was lost in exile, keeping believer's eyes on the horizon to look for the Seed of the woman who would crush the serpent's head.[7] God administered the covenant of grace under Moses very differently from how he does now, yet this covenant was the covenant of grace and not the covenant of works. Even the built-in defects of the Mosaic covenant are God's blessings to us because they lead us to Christ without letting us be satisfied with Moses.

## David

Key parts of J. R. R. Tolkien's *Lord of the Rings* echo the Davidic covenant. Great kings once reigned from Numenor, but the character of the kings diminished, and the kingdom declined. Almost disappearing, the line of kings continued nonetheless, though without crown and throne. When Aragorn appeared, he had no form or comeliness making him desirable. Yet in him the kingdom revived with the long-awaited king reigning and bringing healing and peace to Middle Earth.

Tolkien's story is a mirror image of the Davidic covenant. Beginning with David, this covenant declined gradually toward exile and the loss of the kingdom, to restoration and hope without restoring king and kingdom, leading to Christ's reign as the true king. David was the last stage of the covenant of grace before Christ came.

7 This is what the book of Hebrews is about, especially chapters 7–10, which we will return to in the next chapter.

As with the covenants of redemption, works, and grace (in Genesis 3:15), the term *covenant* does not appear in 2 Samuel 7, where God revealed it to David. It appears only later, when David celebrated the covenant, in places like Psalm 89 and 132. This reminds us that covenant theology is more about finding the thing than reading the express words.

David wanted to build a house, or temple, for God, showing the permanence of God's covenant presence among his people. While the Lord commanded Moses to build a tent, David took the initiative to build him a house. God responded that David would not build such a "house," though his son Solomon would. Instead, the Lord would build a "house" for David, ensuring that he would always have a son as heir until the Seed of the woman came.[8] Faith leading to obedience remained the condition of the Davidic covenant, sanctioning and rejecting those who did not believe, repent, and obey. Passages like 2 Samuel 7 and Psalms 89 and 132 are the reason why later books like 2 Chronicles show repeatedly that God preserved the line of David, in spite of the sins of his sons. While the northern kings in Israel rarely had dynasties lasting even a few generations, David's line never broke, though sometimes it was reduced to one descendant. Like Aragorn, the line of kings remained intact until the true King inherited the throne. God's faithful covenant keeping with David and his family is a blessed reassurance that God will never forget his covenant with us in Christ.

There is too much to say here about the Davidic covenant. This final and fullest stage of the covenant of grace in the Old Testament dominated the minds of believers, especially in the Psalms and Prophets, making them long for the return of the king. Yet the return of the king

---

8  The words "Seed of the woman" are not explicit in the chapters I am citing. I am using the phrase because it connects the unified story of the Bible by connecting key ideas.

proved to be a coming more than a mere return. The Son of David was the Seed of the woman, the God of judgment and salvation, the one bringing the blessing of Abraham, the prophet like Moses, and so much more. Zechariah's prayer at the birth of his son, John the Baptist, illustrates how David's covenant tied together the majestic unity of the covenant of grace under the Old Testament:

Blessed be the Lord God of Israel,
    for he has visited and redeemed his people
and has raised up a horn of salvation for us
    in the house of his servant David,
as he spoke by the mouth of his holy prophets from of old,
that we should be saved from our enemies
    and from the hand of all who hate us;
to show the mercy promised to our fathers
    and to remember his holy covenant,
the oath that he swore to our father Abraham, to grant us
    that we, being delivered from the hand of our enemies,
might serve him without fear,
    in holiness and righteousness before him all our days.
And you, child, will be called the prophet of the Most High;
    for you will go before the Lord to prepare his ways,
to give knowledge of salvation to his people
    in the forgiveness of their sins,
because of the tender mercy of our God,
    whereby the sunrise shall visit us from on high
to give light to those who sit in darkness and in the shadow of
        death,
    to guide our feet into the way of peace. (Luke 1:68–79)

This glorious summary does not include every stage of the covenant of grace, yet does it need to if the covenant constitutes the breathtaking unity of Scripture? Are we not starting to see a beautiful seamless pattern in the Bible? From Adam to Christ, the Seed of the woman would save his seed by crushing the serpent's head, sealing his promises to them in sacraments.

## Christ

Like children portioning off favorite foods at mealtime, the Bible saves the "best for last." Christ's coming is the final installment of the covenant of grace until the world ends. His death established a covenant that is at once both "new" and final (Matt. 26:28, ESV margin note). Unsurprisingly, God embedded the promises of this covenant in a sacrament at the Last Supper, signifying and sealing it through bread and wine. As Christ drew the Lord's Supper from part of the Last Supper, the Lord's Supper not only points to the best part of the meal; it makes us guests at God's table.

In the "new covenant" the Seed of the woman crushed the serpent's head, delivering us from sin and its consequences. The ways in which Christ as the main theme of God's symphony ties together all the parts is far-reaching and almost overwhelming. He is the Seed of Abraham (Gal. 3:16), the Prophet like Moses (Acts 3:22), and David's Son and Lord (Matt. 22:45). Above all, he is Priest, offering himself for our sins, and interceding for us forever. The Noahic covenant continues for his sake, preserving the world while God calls his elect (2 Pet. 3:9). He is fully God in true human flesh (Phil. 2:5–8), humbling himself to exalt us that we might be humbled by his exaltation (Phil. 2:9–11; John 17; Heb. 7:25). He is "Immanuel" (Isa. 7:14), bringing God's presence to his people in the "temple" of his body (John 2:21). Jesus blesses the children and infants of believers (Matt. 19:13–15; Mark 10:13–16; Luke 18:15), bringing "the blessing of Abraham" to their households (Luke 19:9; Gal. 3:14). In short, he is the substance of the covenant of grace, requiring repentance and baptism, giving promises to believers and their children, and saving the nations (Acts 2:38; Isa. 42:6).

The Son, the seed, and the sacraments run through the covenant of grace from Genesis 3:15 to Christ, unifying the Bible in a way that should fill us with awe and wonder at God. We must become parties of the covenant of grace through faith and union with Christ. We can't know God without him. We must lay hold of God's redemptive promises in Jesus Christ. Without the condition of faith, which Christ gives us through his Spirit, we remain under the sanctions of the covenant of works by neglecting the covenant of grace. While it takes prayer, time, and toil to apply the covenant of grace to every part of the Bible, are you beginning to see the breathtaking unity of Scripture? Like a diverse group of friends with different skin colors, accents, families, and cultures, every part of Scripture shares a common story.

## Questions

1. How can the Son, the seed, and the sacraments help us understand the covenant of grace from Adam to Christ?

2. Why is the Noahic covenant part of the covenant of grace? Have you heard people describe this covenant in other ways? What difference does this make?

3. What does the Abrahamic covenant have to do with God's promises to families? Does this have any relevance to believers under the new covenant?

4. Why is the Mosaic covenant more debated than other stages of the covenant of grace? What leads us to think that it still belongs to the covenant of grace?

5. How did the Davidic covenant prepare the way for the new covenant?

3

# Covenant, Testament, and Joyful Bible Reading

LONGTIME CHRISTIANS can take it for granted how hard Bible reading can be (or once was). For example, when I became a Christian, I got hung up on the table of contents. Why, for example, was this book divided into the Old and New Testaments? The most that people could tell me was that one part looked ahead to Christ's coming and the other looked back on what he did. Yet why the title "testament," and who made this term the dividing line between Malachi and Matthew? I learned later that the Old and New Testaments were a matter of covenant theology. A testament was a special kind of covenant, stressing an inheritance coming after someone died via his or her last will (Heb. 9:15–17, but more about this later). Both the Old and New Testaments hinge on Christ's death, which fulfilled the old covenant, replacing it with the new. Covenant theology proved to be the blessing I needed to understand not just the contents of the Bible but even its table of contents. And what can be more basic than understanding a table of contents?

How we understand the old and new covenants and Testaments raises lots of practical questions: Is the Old Testament relevant to Christians? Do we still need to keep the Ten Commandments (which I also found to be absent from the table of contents)? Are children included in the new covenant? Did the Holy Spirit work in the Old Testament, and if so, how? Though some of these questions need to wait for the last section in this book, this chapter cuts through the mud a bit by explaining the basics of the old and new covenants and Testaments. Alongside other texts, the book of Hebrews offers us a lot of help in this direction. Particularly, showing why the new covenant (in the New Testament) is better than the old can help us see the blessings of covenant theology even more clearly without losing the unity of the Bible. Because the idea of covenants is primary, it comes before testaments in this chapter.

## Old and New Covenant

First, in general, the new covenant is better than the old. We pick up on this idea even through surface Bible reading. Yet what is the old covenant? Closely related, how does the old covenant relate to "the law"? When the New Testament refers to the law as a covenant, sometimes it implies the law's use in the covenant of works (Rom. 3:20; Gal. 2:16; 4:25). In other words, sometimes the law illustrates how much trouble we are in without the gospel. Yet commonly, the law refers to the Mosaic covenant as the legal administration of the covenant of grace (2 Cor. 3:7–18). In this case, the law does not so much oppose the gospel as it contrasts promise and fulfillment. As John put it, "For the law was given through Moses; grace and truth came through Jesus Christ" (John 1:17). Christ cast his shadow through the old covenant, but when he brought God's grace and truth in bodily form, the shadow disappears (Col. 2:17).[1] Most of the time, the New Testament refers to the old covenant as the Old Testament administration of the covenant of grace, with special emphasis on Moses.

How is the new covenant better than the old? Without going into every detail, Hebrews illustrates some differences between the two. This is where our themes of the Son, the seed, and the sacraments can help us hear the same message in both covenants without becoming deaf to the dramatic changes in the music. The Son himself was the primary promise of the covenant of grace to the seed (the church). In this light, what we learned above about the sacraments of the covenant of grace under Moses being defective by design helps us understand why the new is better. Only Christ can save his people from their sins. God designed temporary, bloody, repeated sacraments under the old covenant to remind his church of this fact. Priests offering sacrifices on an altar at a temple—daily, yearly, and generationally—are gone forever. This is one of the main points of Hebrews, in which the "old covenant" almost always has the Mosaic covenant in view. The sacraments of the old covenant were temporary because Christ had to come, and we need him desperately.

Some examples from Hebrews show this clearly. Under the old covenant, priests were defective in that they had to sacrifice for their own sins before making offering for the sins of others (Heb. 5:3; 7:27). They were impermanent because their deaths prevented them from continuing to be priests (7:23). Sacrifices were repeated daily and yearly, showing that they could not ultimately take away sins (10:11); only Christ could do this. The tabernacle, signifying God's covenant presence, was only a copy of the heavenly pattern that God showed

---

1    The Greek text of this verse makes the contrast between shadow and body clearer than English translations usually convey.

Moses (8:5). Christ removed all these bloody sacraments because he fulfilled them. He was sinless and undefiled, needing no sacrifice for his own sins (7:26). Jesus is a priest forever (7:17), who always lives and intercedes for us (7:25). Offering himself once, he perfects forever those who are being sanctified as his people (10:14). Christ is minister in the true and heavenly tabernacle, not the man-made copy (8:2). Reading the old covenant through new covenant glasses, we can see clearly rather than squint vaguely at the body casting his shadow through these old covenant pictures. We should bless God that we no longer need to wonder what God's fulfillment of all these things would look like. We have the same gospel that believers did under the old covenant but written more clearly, in larger characters, and read more easily.

None of this implies that the Mosaic covenant, or old covenant, was not the covenant of grace. Yet the new covenant marked a drastic change in administering the covenant of grace, so seismic in proportions that it was like shaking heaven and earth (Hag. 2:6; Heb. 12:26). The new covenant made the old "obsolete" and ready to pass away (Heb. 8:13). It is hard for us to appreciate the trauma that Jewish Christians went through in moving from the old covenant to the new. No more temple, no more priests, no more sacrifices, no more pilgrimages to Jerusalem, no more food laws, and no more mostly Jewish church. Can we see why some Jewish Christians were tempted to go back? Some Jewish leaders were so enraged by these radical changes that they murdered Stephen in Acts 7 on charges of teaching that Jesus would destroy the temple and change the "customs" of Moses (Acts 6:14).

Now God administers his promises about Christ through the word and by the sacraments of baptism and the Lord's Supper. This is why new covenant worship looks so simple, bordering mundane. We don't have temples, priests, incense, altars, and outward pomp. Though God previously commanded such things, he now forbids them because old covenant worship expired with Christ's finished work. Yet the astonishing reality is that saints under the old covenant received less of God through more ordinances than we do through less. The chapter on the Trinity below helps explain why. In the meantime, when we arrive to church Sunday morning tired, with crying or fighting children, wondering whether we have to talk to the awkward visitor, in an old building, with no smells, bells, and whistles, we should never lose sight of the glory of God's covenant presence among us. We worship by faith and not by sight. Would we rather have a taste of the outward glory of old covenant worship and less of God in it, or less outward glory and much more of the Lord? We should put our hearts in check whenever we act like we long for old covenant forms of worship more than the Spirit's inward power under the new covenant.

Second, specifically, the new covenant is better than the old in its spiritual power and reach. Emphasizing the superiority of the new covenant over the old, the author of Hebrews quoted Jeremiah 31:31–34:

> Behold, the days are coming, declares the Lord,
>> when I will establish a new covenant with the house of Israel
>> and with the house of Judah,
> not like the covenant that I made with their fathers
>> on the day when I took them by the hand to bring them out of
>> the land of Egypt.
> For they did not continue in my covenant,

and so I showed no concern for them, declares the Lord.

For this is the covenant that I will make with the house of Israel
    after those days, declares the Lord:

I will put my laws into their minds,
    and write them on their hearts,

and I will be their God,
    and they shall be my people.

And they shall not teach, each one his neighbor
    and each one his brother, saying, "Know the Lord,"

for they shall all know me,
    from the least of them to the greatest.

For I will be merciful toward their iniquities,
    and I will remember their sins no more. (Heb. 8:8–12)

The author primarily stressed the phrase, "I will remember their sins no more." Why? "The law," with its priests, sacrifice, and temple, made nothing "perfect" (Heb. 7:19). Only Christ brings perfect and complete salvation. The law came through Moses, pointing to Christ, but Christ alone brings "grace and truth" to his people through his finished work (John 1:17).[2] The "new covenant" is "not like" the old, specifically in that God would put his law in his people's minds and hearts, that he would be their God with them as his people, that they would all know the Lord from "the least of them to the greatest," and that their sins would be forgiven. While doubtless the superior power and effectiveness of the new covenant are in view, it is easy to assume too much about what this text means and what it does not.

---

2  The question-and-answer chapter below shows that "grace and truth" in John 1 allude to the Hebrew words *chesed* and *emet*, which are Old Testament covenant terms describing God's "steadfast love" and "faithfulness" in covenant with his people.

For example, many of my Baptist friends assume an absolute contrast between the old and new covenants. They believe that, in contrast to the old covenant, the Lord writes his law on the hearts of everyone in the new covenant, with the result that everyone in the new covenant knows the Lord. This is why the new covenant is "not like" the old, which the people "broke." Among other things, they add that this means that while God included children in the old covenant, he no longer does so in the new. Only those who are born of the Spirit are part of the covenant because they alone know the Lord and have the law in their hearts. Thus, children cannot be members of the covenant, and infant baptism does not replace infant circumcision. While largely ignoring questions about infant—or perhaps better, household—baptism here, this absolute contrast raises problems. Identifying and solving them can help explain the relationship between the old and new covenants better.

What are the problems with making an absolute contrast between the old and new covenants? Sidestepping for a moment the promise that all shall know the Lord, the other details of the passage give clues that most of the contrasts in the passage are relative rather than absolute. For example, God being our God and we being his people, with him dwelling among us, was always the core promise of the covenant of grace. Though Christ's coming alone makes this promise possible, there is nothing fundamentally new here. What about the forgiveness of sins? While it is true that Christ's death is necessary for forgiveness before God, David celebrated being the person whose sins were forgiven in Psalms like 32 and 51. Forgiveness was an Old Testament experience based on future realities. God was merciful to the iniquities of old covenant saints, not remembering their sins (Ps. 103:12) and casting them into the depths of the sea (Mic. 7:19) as they waited for Christ to come. What about having the law written on the heart? Again, did not God promise to circumcise the hearts of believers and their children so that they might love him and keep his commandments (Deut. 30:6)? It is hard to imagine the author of Psalm 119 extolling God's law from an uncircumcised heart (e.g., Ps. 119:10–11, 32, 36, 58, 77, 92, 97, 112, 174). The faithful remnant, though a minority in Israel, had the law in their hearts too (Isa. 51:7). Concerning the Old Testament believer, the psalmist wrote that because "the law of his God is in his heart; / his steps do not slip" (Ps. 37:31). Those wanting to make an absolute contrast between the benefits of the old covenant and the new, defining the new covenant church in terms of the only people who are born again, need to look at the price tag of their teaching. Would we really want to say that old covenant believers were not forgiven, did not have the Spirit's work and the law in their hearts, and did not have God dwelling among them? Doesn't this "prove" too much?

Scripture instead leads us to conclude that the contrast between the old and new covenants is relative in some respects, and absolute in others. The new covenant is not substantially different from the old. God's covenant presence in Christ and the Spirit's work in believers' hearts are essentially the same in both. However, this point should not undermine the stark contrast between the efficacy and power of the new covenant and the old. Under the old covenant, people looked to Christ to come, but he had not yet come; God forgave their sins, though Christ had not yet purchased redemption; very few people had the law in their hearts, and now many more do; few knew the Lord, and now all classes of people from all nations know the Lord "from the least to the greatest." Peter seemed to understand such new covenant promises in this way, quoting Joel 2 in Acts 2:17–21 to show how far and wide the power and reach of the new covenant was. It is a mistake to try to understand "they shall all know me from the least to the greatest" in one new covenant text without including others like it. Christ's work under the new covenant was so great that it would not leave room for the old covenant anymore, and the Spirit's work is so powerful under the new covenant that it is as though he had done nothing up to this point (John 7:37–39). Also, can anyone admit people to the new covenant church on the grounds of spiritual rebirth when we cannot see the heart? Peter baptized Simon the sorcerer when he professed faith in Christ (Acts 8:13), though Peter later concluded that he was not born again (8:21). All of us baptize people because they belong to the covenant, not because they have the Spirit in their hearts.

The work of Christ and the work of the Spirit under the new covenant brought the church into a new era. Greater revelation of the Savior brought greater power of the Spirit, both in preaching and in Christian living.[3] The Spirit has, as it were, greater tools to work with as we have a clearer picture of Christ for him to copy into our lives through writing God's law on our hearts. Likewise, if we really want to grow in holiness, or in likeness to God's holy character, then we need to get to know Jesus Christ as well as possible, since the Spirit is making us like him. More people know the Lord now, and they know him better than old covenant saints ever could. God's promises to believers are broader and better, not narrower and worse, than they were under the old covenant. God is not merely among us; he is within us. We would do well to live up to our privileges by studying the Bible prayerfully and daily, loving new covenant worship on the Lord's Day, and by expecting the Spirit to bless our fight against sin and our pursuit of Christ's character. God's new covenant promises

---

3  I treat the question regarding whether the Spirit indwelled believers in the Old Testament in the questions toward the end of this book.

belong to us, to our children, and to as many as are afar off whom the Lord our God will call (Acts 2:39).

## Old and New Testament

But what do we do with the table of contents in our Bibles? What about the Old and New Testaments? Put simply, the Old and New Testaments largely divide our Bibles between the covenant of grace in its old and new covenant administrations.

What is a *testament*? A testament is a last will, in which someone who dies assigns his or her possessions to people as his or her heirs. We still refer to last wills and testaments when we decide who receives our possessions when we die. Older authors believed that all testaments were covenants, though not all covenants were testaments. The conditions in testaments were more one-sided than other covenants since they rested on the will and disposition of the one who died. This is why when Christ offered himself to the Father by the eternal Spirit, Hebrews 9:14–17 argues that the new covenant is like a last will and testament through which Jesus brought his people an eternal inheritance.

Because Christ's death and our inheritance are so central to the new covenant, the authors of the Westminster Confession of Faith concluded that "this covenant of grace is frequently set forth in Scripture by the name of a testament."[4] The Greek word standing behind our English word "covenant" is the same for "testament." Yet this statement in the Confession is not a justification for how often the translators of the King James Version used "testament" instead of "covenant." The point is that the new covenant is a testamentary covenant resting on Christ's death.[5] As a result, the Old Testament tells us what Christ

---

4   WCF 7.4 (*CCC* 196).

5   The questions in the last section of this book explore this issue a bit more.

would do to purchase our inheritance, while the New Testament shows us the inheritance he purchased by his death. We celebrate the New Testament every time we observe the Lord's Supper because the New Testament marks the new covenant in Christ's blood.

Though Jesus used this language at the Last Supper, the New Testament begins with his death. John the Baptist was the last and greatest Old Testament prophet, no longer telling people about the coming Christ but pointing the finger at him who had come. When Jesus finished his work, he closed the final chapter of the Old Testament by turning to the New, which is the final chapter of God's book. Pulling together the Old Testament and New Testament in light of what we have seen about the old and new covenants, Westminster Larger Catechism questions 34–35 summarize both the unity of and changes within the covenant of grace from the Old to the New Testament:

> The covenant of grace was administered under the old testament, by promises, prophecies, sacrifices, circumcision, the Passover, and other types and ordinances, which did all foresignify Christ then to come, and were for that time sufficient to build up the elect in faith in the promised Messiah, by whom they then had full remission of sin, and eternal salvation.[6]

And,

> Under the new testament, when Christ the substance was exhibited, the same covenant of grace was and still is to be administered in the preaching of the Word, and the administration of the sacraments

6    WLC q. 34 (*CCC* 346).

of baptism and the Lord's Supper; in which grace and salvation are held forth in more fullness, evidence, and efficacy, to all nations.[7]

God is our God and the God of our seed in covenant, we are his people, and he dwells among us. This was God's plan in the covenant of redemption, this is what Adam lost in the covenant of works, and this is what Christ reclaimed and expanded in the covenant of grace. Hopefully, this helps us not only understand the table of contents in our Bibles but also read the Bible with spiritual joy by seeing Christ as its theme on every page. The Son, the seed, and the sacraments are key ideas to help us do this.

## Covenants and Reading the Bible with Spiritual Joy

Bible reading can be hard, even when we get past the table of contents. Proverbially, people who start reading the Bible quit in Leviticus, not knowing what to do with the priests, sacrifices, and many other details. Yet the faithful few who keep going usually get hung up again with books like Chronicles. Whether or not we understand them well, we should love the whole Bible because our Father in heaven lovingly gave us precisely the words we need, as the Spirit leads us to Christ. We should enjoy God's words as a child treasures a letter from a father deployed overseas. Yet the more we understand God's words, the more we enjoy them. Covenant theology teaches us to read the Bible with spiritual joy as we see the breathtaking unity of God's message, revolving around Christ, the Seed of the woman, in at least two ways.

First, covenant theology helps us grasp the Bible's central message. Here I summarize Westminster Confession chapter 7 to illustrate the

7 WLC q. 35 (CCC 346).

point. This is what the story looks like: Before he made the world, God planned to send Jesus to save his people from their sins, and to send his Spirit to bring them to the Savior. Though mankind should have obeyed God simply because he is God, God promised the reward of eternal life to Adam and Eve if they persevered. As soon as the first couple sinned against God, the Lord promised to save his people through the Seed of the woman, who would undo the sin and misery that Satan introduced to humanity. This covenant rests on Christ alone, giving believers a sure eternal inheritance in and through himself. The triune God revealed this covenant gradually in the "time of the law" under Adam, Noah, Abraham, Moses, and David, making his promises in Christ clearer every step of the way.[8]

Living in "the time of the gospel," God shows us Christ more clearly and fully, who purchased our salvation, and who gives us the Holy Spirit to bring us to God.[9] God dwells within us and not merely among us. Just as God gave his covenants through word and sacrament then, so now he continues to present his gracious covenant to us through the preaching of the word, baptism, and the Lord's Supper. Through these, he teaches us both how to read our Bibles and where to meet Christ, leading us to grasp his promises through faith. Even retelling the Bible's story in this way should make our hearts leap for joy in the Spirit! Does this not help us summarize the gospel as well, which is the core of the Bible's covenantal story? Our evangelism can become more like telling a gripping story than giving people a dry list of doctrines.

Second, covenant theology produces spiritual joy by helping us understand the parts of Scripture. Some things in the Bible are "hard to understand" (2 Pet. 3:16). Unravelling some questions requires fervent

8   WCF 7.5 (CCC 196).
9   WCF 7.5 (CCC 196).

prayer for wisdom and hard work in study. Yet covenant theology sets our questions in the right context. It is much easier to read Chronicles with Genesis 3:15 handy than it is to stumble through a list of names. Genealogies are covenant history, separating the woman's seed from the serpent's seed, and lead us to Christ. Likewise, Leviticus makes a lot more sense with the covenant theology of Hebrews in view. Difficult questions surrounding the Mosaic covenant become resolvable by keeping Abraham's covenant in view. How you understand the whole Bible, with Christ at its center, will always help you learn to enjoy the parts better, increasing your joy in the Spirit as you grow in knowing God.

Covenant theology can serve as a key to unlock and enjoy the riches stored in every book of Scripture. Reading the Bible while asking what it tells you about God, how it points to Christ, and how you relate to him in covenant should be radically transformative. Take in the breathtaking unity of Scripture on its own covenant terms and cultivate the joy of the Spirit as you take up and read—and keep rereading.

## Questions

1. Why is the Bible divided into the Old and New Testaments? How can covenant theology help you explain why this is the case?

2. How is the new covenant better than the old covenant? What remains the same, and what is different?

3. What is a testament, and how are testaments related to covenants? Why does the testamentary idea dominate the new covenant?

4. Which books of the Bible are most difficult for you? Can you think of ways that covenant theology can help you make sense of some of these difficulties?

5. What should you look for as you read your Bible? How can looking for the right things increase your communion with God through Bible reading?

# Covenant Theology and the Triune God

ONE OF MY FAVORITE TASKS as a church officer is preparing covenant children to publicly profess their faith in Christ. Though most of them are baptized church members, born in Christian families, publicly confessing their faith in Christ is part of their taking ownership of God's covenant promises. Doing so does not necessarily mark their conversion. The Lord brings some of them through crises in which the Spirit leads them to take sin and Christ seriously for the first time. However, like John the Baptist (Luke 1:44), others never know a day when they did not have Spirit-filled love for Christ and joy in him. Covenant children who believe walk different paths, but they reach the same destination. The main thing is that they arrive at knowing Christ for themselves, regardless of how the Spirit leads them there.

Early in the class, I like to ask the children what it means to give a Christian "testimony." People who never knew a day when they did not trust in and love Jesus Christ often get hung up here. When someone gives their testimony, we often expect to hear a dramatic story of how that person came to Christ. Not having a striking conversion experience makes some believers self-conscious, feeling like they are missing something. Because of this fact, I usually tell covenant children two things: first, Jesus is the answer to every question; and second, Christians have different experiences, but we all have the same testimony. Paul was converted dramatically when Christ stopped him in his tracks on the way to Damascus while persecuting the church (Acts 9). Yet Timothy had faith through knowing the Scriptures since childhood (2 Tim. 3:15), growing to trust in Jesus as he learned about him (Acts 16:1–3). Yet both men testified to the same Christ (2 Cor. 4:5), and so must we. Testimonies are about what Christ has done for and to us, not about our life histories, as interesting and relevant as they might be.

What does this have to do with the Trinity and the covenant? Put simply, the gospel is about God, and the more God reveals the gospel through his covenant, the more of God we see and know. The covenant and the gospel are about knowing the right God in the right way. Eternal life is knowing the only true and living God through Christ, who is the only mediator between God and man (John 17:3; 1 Tim. 2:5). Yet no one confesses that Jesus Christ is Lord except by the Holy Spirit (1 Cor. 12:3). As the covenant of grace unfolds gradually, so the glory of the triune God becomes clearer. These are not merely coincidental facts. The highest glory of the new covenant is that we walk in intimate fellowship with the Father, through the Son, by the Spirit. The old covenant prepared us for the full revelation of God as triune, and we cannot understand the new covenant apart from the triune God, who is its chief blessing. We can see this through baptism, through several New Testament gospel summaries, and by rereading the Old Testament through new covenant Trinitarian lenses.

## How Does Baptism as a Covenant Sign Help
## Us Know the Triune God's Glory?

Much like flags are attached to nations, signs are attached to covenants. The flag is not the nation, but it represents the nation. Traditionally flags have distinguished opposing armies in warfare, and people have used T-shirts, tattoos, and other means to mark their national identities with national flags. There are even special rules about how to treat national flags and respectfully dispose of damaged ones, since respecting the flag is an act of respecting the nation it represents.

This is like how sacraments function as covenant signs in the Bible. For example, circumcision "is" God's covenant, though it is only a "sign" of his covenant (Gen. 17:10–11). Sacraments are so closely tied to the promises that they point to, and thus encapsulate the promises of the covenants, that the Bible speaks about the one as though it is the other.[1] We should reach through covenant signs by faith to grasp the thing that they point to—namely, Christ himself. This is why, in the Lord's Supper, Jesus said, "This is my body," while holding ordinary bread, and this cup is the "blood of the new covenant" (NKJV), though holding an ordinary cup in his hands (Matt. 26:26–29). Yet the relationship between the sign and the thing it signifies, or points to, is close. When God's word sets apart ordinary bread and wine for special use in the Lord's Supper, abusing the elements makes us "guilty concerning the body and blood of the Lord" (1 Cor. 11:27). Despising circumcision was covenant breaking (Gen. 17:14), and abusing the Lord's Supper is an attack on Christ (1 Cor. 11:27). Conversely, when we take the sacraments through faith in God's covenant promises, we

---

1 "There is, in every sacrament, a spiritual relation, or sacramental union, between the sign and the thing signified: whence it comes to pass, that the names and effects of the one are attributed to the other." WCF 27.2 (CCC 227).

receive Christ in them and through them. A spiritual relationship exists between covenant signs and covenant promises. We do not merely lay hold of the signs but lay hold of Christ through them. Abusing the signs by trusting in them, instead of in the Christ they point to, is an act of despising Christ.

In baptism, the triune God plants his flag and stakes his claim on us, so to speak. Baptized people belong to the triune God, which is why the church baptizes them in his triune name (Matt. 28:19). Many issues surround baptism, such as who should be baptized, how baptism relates to faith and conversion, where baptism came from, how we should apply the water, and many others. This is not the place to answer these questions.[2] For Trinity and covenant themes, we only need to see how baptism, as a covenant sign, helps us know the glory of the triune God.[3] As a sacrament, baptism reveals the Son saving his seed, bringing a fuller revelation of the Father and the Spirit with him.

Baptism is a covenant sign. We are baptized into the name of the Father, the Son, and the Holy Spirit (Matt. 28:19). This is a loaded statement, every part of which requires explanation. Like the Lord's Supper, baptism is a sign and seal of the new covenant, and the Father gives both to point to Christ and to apply his benefits to believers, in

2 For just a few recent examples, see Robert Letham, *A Christian's Pocket Guide to Baptism: The Water That Unites* (Fearn, UK: Christian Focus, 2012); J. V Fesko, *Word, Water, and Spirit: A Reformed Perspective on Baptism* (Grand Rapids, MI: Reformation Heritage Books, 2010); Jason Helopoulos, *Covenantal Baptism*, Blessings of the Faith (Phillipsburg, NJ: P&R, 2021).

3 See my little book *Does Infant Baptism Matter?* (Grand Rapids, MI: Reformation Heritage Books, 2023). This book argues that baptism is God's word to us, baptism is God's covenant word to us, and baptism is God's covenant word to us and our children. The second half of the book applies baptism to the church, to the family, and to the individual.

the church, to the end of the world. Unlike the Lord's Supper, baptism happens only once, and it points to our initial union with Christ by the Spirit, rather than to our continual communion with him through faith.[4] Like circumcision, baptism stresses more what God says to us in covenant than what we say in response. Put differently, baptism requires faith, but it does not signify faith. God identifies us through baptism as the people he is in covenant with. Just as the central theme of the covenant of grace is God's covenant presence with his people, so the resurrected Christ promised to be with his baptized church to the end of the age (Matt. 28:20). Whether or not we believed when we were baptized, the triune God really said something in baptism, which we would do well to believe.

Baptism is identity shaping. The triune "name" shows us both who owns us and what we should believe. God's "name" revealed in the old covenant was Yahweh, the one who eternally is who he is, and who is willing and able to keep the terms of his covenant (Ex. 3:14). God's "name," not names, revealed in the new covenant is "Father, Son, and Holy Spirit." We will see below that this means that the Father chose to save us, the Son purchased our salvation, and the Spirit applies our salvation, reflecting the covenant of redemption as the foundation of the covenant of grace. These persons are not three gods but the true and living God under a single divine "name." The three personal names do not distinguish their deity from one another but mark their order of subsistence, as the church likes to say, within the Godhead. "Subsistence" is the church's attempt to say that we are dealing with one being with three personal distinctions inherent within God rather than three separate beings or people. "God" is the category (being or

---

4 These two sentences summarize WLC 176–77 (*CCC* 400).

essence) enveloping Father, Son, and Holy Spirit, while "person" points to distinctions, order, and relations within God.

When we think about human persons, we think of individual people who all belong to the category of "human being." Being human is what we have in common; personal distinctions are what we don't. Our personhood dimly reflects God's; he is the perfect original, and we are the imperfect copies. Since there is one God, "persons" refer to distinctions within the category of God. Though hard to grasp, this means that the Son is all that the Father is except Father, and that the Spirit is all that the Father and Son are except Father and Son. Order, relationship, and distinction exist within God, without dividing him into three gods or collapsing the persons into pretended roles. In reality, human persons are odd because we are one kind of being, but divided into distinct individual people. Eternally, God is one God in three persons. He is the perfect original, and we are the imperfect copies. He alone can exist in three persons without dividing himself into people. The wondrous truth is that baptism identifies us with this God as our God, with incalculable implications for the Christian life. Father, Son, and Spirit is his new covenant name.

It is easier to explain how we relate to the triune God than it is to explain who he is. Baptism shows us that we need salvation from the one true God, in the order of from the Father, through the Son, and by the Spirit. We depend on all three persons distinctly as we worship them jointly. We worship them jointly when we depend on all three. No baptized person has the right to reject the terms of the covenant by rejecting Christ. God owns the person, both by creation and by covenant. Put positively, every baptized person has every encouragement to receive and rest in the promises of the triune God that are signified and sealed in baptism. The sacrament leads us to be God's seed through faith in his Son.

As a covenant sign, baptism not only carries promises but also makes demands. Baptism requires our self-identification with God. Water in baptism shows us that we need washing. We wash things, like piles of laundry, that are dirty. Due to the filthiness of our sins, we need to be washed by Christ's blood (1 John 1:7), and we need to be washed by the Spirit's regenerating power (Titus 3:5). When we receive the Spirit, God adopts us into his family in Christ (Gal. 4:4–7). Baptism highlights the glory of the new covenant by embedding the Trinity into the sign of entrance into the new covenant church. We also hope to dwell with the triune God at the resurrection. This has lifelong significance, reminding people who have been baptized into Christ that they have put on Christ (Gal. 3:27), that baptism identifies them with his death and resurrection (Rom. 6:3–4), and that they should no longer live for themselves (Rom. 6:5–14). Rather than presupposing faith in a momentary confession, baptism requires and encourages faith that lasts a lifetime. The church does not baptize innocent people, whether infants or adults. Declaring that people are filthy and need washing, baptism presses us to come to the Father, through the Son, by the Spirit. Baptism brings God and man as covenanting parties together in fellowship, as Christ's seed lays hold of his covenant promises through faith. Revealing the glory of God as triune, baptism strengthens covenant obligations without exhausting them.

Baptism is a better sign than any old covenant sign could be. The new covenant is founded on better promises (Heb. 8:6), revealing God's name better to us than the old covenant saints knew. This means that baptism always presses us toward the completion of the covenant of grace and toward a greater knowledge of the God who dwells in us and not only among us. Only seeing the triune God in heaven can fully satisfy this desire. While the church sometimes neglects the importance of the Trinity, covenantal baptism never lets us get away from him fully. Even where Christians have forgotten why the Trinity is so important for Christian faith and life, baptism forces us to talk about the Trinity on some level every time we witness it. The gospel is about God's saving work more than it is about a list of benefits that he gives us. Baptism places a Trinitarian flag in every Christian person and in every Christian church, setting the glory of the new covenant on display, revealing God gloriously. In baptism, the Son and the seed come together through a sacrament, by the Spirit's power, to the Father's glory.

## How Do New Covenant Gospel Summaries Help Us Know the Triune God's Glory?

My family and I travel a lot. When we go to other English-speaking countries, or sometimes even parts of America, the first thing people notice is our generic American (California in my case) accents. Everything we say reflects who we are and where we are from. Likewise, the Trinity is the accent of the new covenant, standing behind almost everything in the New Testament. The apostles could hardly speak about the gospel or the Christian life without rooting both in the Father, Son, and Holy Spirit, illustrating once again that knowing God as triune is the central focus and blessing of the new covenant.

Citing "covenant" texts is not really necessary here, since we have already established that the New Testament is about the new covenant administration of the covenant of grace. The God who is our God is the centerpiece of the covenant, and he shines forth most clearly in the new covenant. This is why the Trinity has always been the heart of the gospel throughout church history, especially in the early church. Several examples illustrating the Trinitarian accent of the New Testament push us to know and think in terms of the triune God in everything.[5]

Ephesians 2:18 is a good place to start: "For through him we both have access in one Spirit to the Father." The church's covenant communion with God is inescapably Trinitarian. The covenant of grace is about the nations knowing God through the Seed of the woman. Here Paul tells Jews and Gentiles ("we both have access") in the Christian church that in "one Spirit," through Jesus Christ, they come to the Father. They who were "strangers to the covenants of promise" (2:12) are now brought near to the triune God through Christ's blood. The covenant promises that God should be our God and we his people find their fulfillment through all kinds of people coming to the Father, through the Son, by the Spirit. In Abraham's Seed, truly all nations are blessed through the church. From the least to the greatest, whoever we are and wherever we are from, we all know God as triune.

The foundations of our faith are Trinitarian. Backing up a bit, Ephesians 1:3–14 praises the Father for choosing us for salvation, sending his Son to purchase our redemption by his blood, and sending the

5  I have written many books (and articles not listed here), both academic and "popular," about the vital importance of the Trinity in Christian faith and practice. For examples, see Ryan M. McGraw, *A Heavenly Directory: Trinitarian Piety, Public Worship, and a Reassessment of John Owen's Theology*, Reformed Historical Theology 29 (Göttingen: Vandenhoeck & Ruprecht, 2014); McGraw, *The Foundation of Communion with God: The Trinitarian Piety of John Owen*, Profiles in Reformed Spirituality (Grand Rapids, MI: Reformation Heritage Books, 2014); McGraw, *John Owen: Trajectories in Reformed Orthodox Theology* (Cham, Switzerland: Palgrave Macmillan, 2017); McGraw, *Is the Trinity Practical?* (Grand Rapids, MI: Reformation Heritage Books, 2016); McGraw, *Knowing the Trinity: Practical Thoughts for Daily Life* (Lancaster, PA: Alliance of Confessing Evangelicals, 2017); and McGraw, *A Mystery Revealed: 31 Meditations on the Triune God* (Grand Rapids, MI: Reformation Heritage Books, 2023).

Spirit as a seal and down payment of heaven. As with baptism, by faith we look to our inheritance in God's family, in Christ, by the Spirit. This gospel doxology reflects the Trinitarian foundations of the covenant of redemption, bearing fruit in the covenant of grace. Such Trinitarian gospel summaries are the substance of the new covenant's message of salvation. Though the term *covenant* does not always appear in some texts explicitly, the divine author of Scripture expects that we are still tracking with the story at this point.

Our prayers are Trinitarian. We address "our Father" in heaven (Matt. 6:9), we ask in Jesus's name (John 14:13), and we pray in the Spirit (Eph. 6:18; Jude 20) and for the Spirit (Luke 11:13). Westminster Larger Catechism 178 puts it well: "Prayer is an offering up of our desires unto God, in the name of Christ, by the help of his Spirit; with confession of our sins, and thankful acknowledgment of his mercies."[6] Such intimate communion with God in prayer is one of the primary fruits of the new covenant. When we pray to the Father, in Jesus's name, in and for the Spirit, we depend on and worship all three persons of the one true Godhead. Drawing from New Testament instructions about prayer, we likely know and practice Trinitarian prayer already, whether or not we are conscious of it. The Trinitarian character of the new covenant is the reason why.

The church, as the product of the new covenant, is Trinitarian too. Describing the church, which is founded on the covenant of grace, Paul wrote that Christians are

members of the household of God, built on the foundation of the apostles and prophets, Christ Jesus himself being the cornerstone, in

6 WLC q. 178 (*CCC* 401).

whom the whole structure, being joined together, grows into a holy temple in the Lord. In him you also are being built together into a dwelling place for God by the Spirit. (Eph. 2:19–22)

The temple embodied God's promises in the old covenant, with God dwelling among his people. Indwelling remains the central promise of the new covenant, with the triune God dwelling within his people. God gave his covenant word through the apostles and prophets, and he founded Christ's new covenant church on their words. Should it surprise us that the nature of the church reflects its foundation in the triune God? The new covenant church coheres in the Trinity (see also Eph. 4:1–6).

The church's covenant signs, or sacraments, are rooted in the Trinity. We have already seen the covenant and the Trinity in baptism. Westminster Larger Catechism 165 reminds us that baptism points to and seals our forgiveness of sins through union with Christ, the Spirit's regenerating power, and our adoption into God's family. What about the Lord's Supper? By definition, the Lord's Supper is "communion" or "participation" in Christ's body and blood (1 Cor. 10:16). In other words, Paul describes the Lord's Supper as fellowship with Jesus. It can't merely be a memorial of Christ because God dwelling with his people always lay at the heart of the covenant of grace. The Lord's Supper is more like sitting at a feast with a friend than it is visiting a cemetery to look at a grave. As we remember Jesus, we meet with him too. This is why when we eat and drink through faith in Christ, we eat and "drink of one Spirit" (1 Cor. 12:13). God spreads us a feast in the Supper so that we might "feed" on Christ by faith (John 6:53), through the Spirit's work in our hearts. Saying that Christ is present in the Spirit in the Supper, bringing God to us and us to God, reemphasizes that God is present personally in the sacrament of the new covenant in Christ's blood (Matt. 26:28). Much like our communion with the triune God in general, it is easier to experience this reality than to describe or explain it.

In short, the Trinitarian texture of the new covenant shows how we have more intimate fellowship with God, than either Adam could before the fall or the old covenant saints could before Christ came and God poured out the Spirit. The beauty of the new covenant is that the central promise of the covenant of grace takes a surprising twist. We do not merely dwell in God's life-giving presence; God takes up residence in our hearts. Relegating the Trinity to a mere definition that God is one in essence and three in persons becomes cold and sterile if we pull the triune God out of the context of covenant communion with us. The Spirit dwells in our hearts, and Christ and his Father make room to dwell there as well (John 14:23). Since God is three persons, we can't have one divine person without the rest. Astonishingly, the triune God dwells within us, drawing us into the intra-Trinitarian life and fellowship. Eternal life is knowing God (John 17:3), and we know him more intimately as triune in the new covenant than anyone could have before Christ came.

## How Can Our New Covenant Knowledge of the Triune God's Glory Help Us Read the Old Testament?

Outstanding authors have a plan. Weaving together seemingly insignificant details into a masterful climax, great stories are best read again. When we reread good stories, we see details we missed the first time because now we know what to look for. Rereading the Old Testament in light of the New Testament helps us better see the triune God's glory, and the triune God's glory helps us profit from the Old Testament. Our covenant fellowship with the triune God sheds light on earlier parts of the story in at least two ways: first, we see how the triune God revealed himself gradually throughout the Old Testament; second, we take our knowledge of the triune God with us as we read the Old Testament.

First, knowing the triune God under the new covenant, we can see traces of him in the old covenant better. The triune God did not reveal himself in the old covenant as clearly as he did in the new. This fact mirrors how "covenant" carries forward the story of Christ's gospel. As the Son, the seed, and the sacraments grow clearer, so does our knowledge of the God who saves us. Though not teaching a full-orbed doctrine of the Trinity, the New Testament view of God would not be possible without the Old Testament. God knew what he was doing every time he spoke. Rereading the stages of the covenant of grace we saw in previous chapters shows how this happened.

Glimpses of the Trinity appear in every stage of covenant history. In the age of the covenant of works, the one God said "let us" make mankind after "our image, after our likeness" (Gen. 1:26), adding, somewhat sarcastically, after Adam broke the covenant, that man had become "like one of us" (3:22). The irony was that through sin, the first couple tried to become more like God, but sin actually made them less like him. Sin always defaces and distorts God's image in us. Yet we should not miss the seeds of Trinitarian teaching here, which would take a long time to grow and bloom fully. God revealed himself as "us" as well as "he," both in the covenant of works and from the outset of the covenant of grace in Genesis 3:15. Can we not at least see God alluding to the fact that he is both "he" and "us," both unity and diversity? Such details may not prove the Trinity, but they anticipate it since the divine author of the Bible knew what he was doing.

Noah's covenant begins with God saying that his "Spirit" would not always strive with man, and that the time of judgment was at hand

(Gen. 6:3). Peter wrote that Christ preached to that generation through Noah, warning them to turn to God (1 Pet. 3:19; 2 Pet. 2:5). Through the Spirit, the Son preached the Father's message through his prophet. This does not mean that Noah would have known this clearly at the time, but in hindsight the pieces start fitting together for us.

Passing by Abraham and Moses for the sake of space, we should begin to see patterns like this in Scripture in light of what the new covenant teaches us about God. Fast-forwarding, under the Davidic covenant, for example, Isaiah's "servant songs," included within Isaiah 42–53, alternate between the Lord and the servant, and the servant and the Spirit. Such details are compatible with the Trinity, without fully revealing the Trinity. Yet is not one of the greatest blessings of living under the new covenant developing the ability to marvel at how God increasingly revealed himself as our triune God and Savior all along?

Lest we think that seeing the Father, Son, and Spirit here, albeit in old covenant shadows, reads too much into the text, Isaiah 59 provides a clear anticipation of the Trinity in the promise of a new covenant. He wrote that the "Redeemer" would come to Zion to turn Jacob from transgression. This "covenant with them" included the Spirit not departing from his people and their children, placing his word in their mouths and hearts, assuring them that the Lord had spoken and would do what he said (Isa. 59:20–21). God promised that the Redeemer would save his people from their sins, putting his word and Spirit in their mouths and hearts for generations. Though many more examples exist, Isaiah's words at least included the Mosaic and Davidic covenants, stressing the law and the anointed King. Without such hints along the way, the new covenant Trinitarian gospel climax would not make good sense.

Like the new covenant Scriptures, Christ is the key to seeing the gradual revelation of the Trinity in the old covenant Scriptures. We see Christ in every prophet, priest, and king, whether through bad examples, which led people to long for him, or through good examples, which direct us to Jesus as the better and best prophet, priest, and king. He "appears" in every sacrifice, in the tabernacle and temple, and in every genealogy, dividing the nations between the seed of the woman and the seed of the serpent. Where Christ is, the Father and the Spirit are always as well, working together with him in breathtaking harmony and indivisible unity. Rereading the Old Testament with new covenant glasses teaches us to get more out of the Old Testament than the old covenant saints could.

Second, we take our new covenant knowledge of the triune God with us when we read the Old Testament. This point is more about how we relate to God under the new covenant than it is about what we find in the Old Testament. For example, it may be easy to see that Psalm 2 revolves around a Father-Son interchange, exalting the Son as King over the nations. Yet what about Psalm 1, which is about the godly man? Is not Christ the true and highest pattern of godly humanity? Should we not ask for the Spirit to make us like Jesus by writing the law on our hearts, as we meditate on it day and night? Likewise, does not every experience of suffering and vindication in the Psalms naturally remind us of Christ's suffering for us and his vindication in his resurrection? In other words, we need to think like Christians in communion with God under the new covenant as we read the old covenant Scriptures. Every rebuke and command in the prophets should lead us to cry out for the Spirit's help, bringing repentance, obedience, and comfort. All God's promises should lead us to faith in Christ, in whom God subsumes and confirms his covenant blessings (2 Cor. 1:20). Likewise, we should treasure all Old Testament texts in the context of calling God Father, who lovingly rebukes and encourages his adopted children (Heb. 12:5–11). This is how the Spirit works in us as we read our Bibles.

In other words, God relates to us through the covenant of grace, and we need to remember our covenant relation to the whole Trinity as we read, preach, hear, and apply old covenant texts.[7] Too often we reduce the gospel to a list of benefits that Christ gives us in place of knowing and glorifying the triune God who dwells within us. Keeping the triune God as the greatest blessing of the covenant of grace before us prevents this. Don't forget what you know about God and how you relate to him as you read the Old Testament. Baptism leads us to testify to Christ as we come to God in the Spirit. The new covenant Scriptures teach us to think about our relationship to God in inescapably Trinitarian terms. Taking these truths with us as we read the Old Testament presses us to know the triune God as our covenant Lord, tincturing everything we think, say, and do with the Trinity.

## Questions

1. What does it mean to give a Christian testimony? How does our testimony differ from and relate to our personal stories?

2. As a covenant sign, how does baptism keep the Trinity central to the gospel? How can baptism help promote communion with the triune God?

---

7 For further examples of applying these principles, see Ryan M. McGraw, *How Shall They Hear? Why Non-Preachers Need to Know What Preaching Is* (Darlington, UK: Evangelical Press, 2019).

3. How do the New Testament authors weave the Trinity into summaries of Christian faith and life? Can you think of other instances beyond those in this chapter in which the New Testament does this?

4. In what ways can your knowledge of the triune God under the new covenant help you read the old?

5. Why does our knowledge of the Trinity in the new covenant deepen our communion with and devotion to God? How does this relate to the central covenant promise that God will dwell among his people as their God?

5

# Covenant Theology and
# the Christian Life

COVENANT THEOLOGY HELPS US see the breathtaking unity of Scripture and know the triune God. Yet how does covenant theology affect our daily lives? Covenant theology changes the way we read our Bibles, but does it change anything else? Viewing God as the central focus and key actor in covenant theology should shape how we think about our relation to God, to others, and to ourselves in everything we do. Keeping covenant theology in view all the time serves to reset our lives by keeping God in his place and us in ours.

Common issues in marriage counseling help illustrate how this works. If you have counseled married couples, or if you are married, then how do marriage problems and conflicts usually take shape? A husband complains that his wife does not respect him, a wife is grieved that her husband is not involved with the children, both husband and wife cannot agree over finances, their sexual relationship is cold and sporadic, and on goes the list. Is there a common thread tying such problems together? Almost every time, how we view our relationship to God in covenant lies at the heart of such problems. How so? Expressing our grievances over our spouses, we come to God and the church to fix our problems when the mess becomes intolerably unmanageable. Yet when we complain about our spouse or our circumstances, instead of starting with God and our responsibilities, we invert the order of the covenant of grace. Though we may not realize it, sin teaches us "me first," then others, and God last because, after all, maybe he can clean up our messes and fix what annoys us in other people. However, the covenant of grace teaches us the triune God first, then others, and then ourselves last, if there is room or time for us.

Many marriage problems start resolving only when people turn the order of our covenant relationship to God right side up instead of upside down. Covenant theology is a blessed means of teaching us how to live the Christian life, especially with others, precisely because the triune God is always first, then his church, and then individuals. We can see how this works further by applying the blessings of covenant theology to the church, to the family, and to the Christian, in that vital and irreversible order.

## How Does Covenant Theology Teach Us to Live in the Church?

Covenant theology means that the church has priority over the individual. Saying so may raise many people's hackles. Don't we need to be born again to enter God's kingdom? Can't we be church members and not have genuine faith in Christ? Don't previous chapters lead us to believe that we need to know the triune God individually and personally if we hope to be saved in the covenant of grace?

Of course, such things are true, but just because salvation is an individual affair does not mean that you are more important than the church. The church is the object of the covenant of redemption, Adam ruined an entire people under the covenant of works, and the covenant of grace separates Christ's seed from Satan's seed. This is why the Son, the seed, and the sacraments have been useful categories to explain God's covenants in the Bible. Because Christ and the church are first in God's plan, we should esteem fellow believers better than ourselves (Phil. 2:3–4). Doesn't Paul argue that this is exactly what Christ did (Phil. 2:5–11), which is why we should do it (Phil. 2:1–4)? Covenant theology kills self-centeredness, fostering genuine Christianity.

For instance, it is impossible to obey most of God's commands in the New Testament by ourselves. How can you be patient, forgiving, kind, long-suffering, and gentle and use your speech and your possessions for good if believing in Christ and reading your Bible are enough? How can you enjoy God's covenant presence in worship (Ps. 100:4) if you forsake assembling yourselves together (Heb. 10:25)? How can you edify others, or be edified by them, if you sing psalms, hymns, and spiritual songs only by yourself (Eph. 5:19; Col. 3:16)? Knowing the triune God personally is always the beginning of the Christian life, but it is never the end. Again, the covenant of grace reminds us that God comes first, then comes the church, and we come last. At the resurrection, to which God's covenant is leading us, the greatest blessing is seeing the triune God as the whole church gathers in exuberant praise. This is why it is God's will that we give ourselves first to God and then to others in this life (2 Cor. 8:5).

Thankfully, God gave the church two covenant signs to illustrate the priority of the church in the Christian life, since their meaning is both Christ centered and church oriented. Let's turn to baptism and the Lord's Supper again. First Corinthians illustrates what goes wrong when sacraments come to be about individuals instead of the church. The Corinthians abused baptism by making it an individual affair and arguing over who had the best baptism by the best ministers (1 Cor. 1:10–17). Unsurprisingly, their so-called devotion masked selfishness when they took the Lord's Supper too, with some people full and drunk, while others had nothing (1 Cor. 11:21). When we distort one covenant sign, twisting into individual rather than corporate meanings, then the other usually goes with it. Any time baptism and the Lord's Supper become more about our personal professions of faith than about God's promises to the church, then something has gone terribly wrong in our understanding of the covenant of grace. How we use the signs illustrates the point. Without intending so, we have made the sacraments, and the covenant by extension, all about us rather than primarily about God and his church.

Paul's correctives to such problems reorient us toward the role of the church in the covenant of grace. He reminded the Corinthians that they were all baptized "in one Spirit" into "one body" (1 Cor. 12:13). Ephesians 4:1–7 similarly urges believers to walk "worthy" of their calling, maintaining "the unity of the Spirit in the bond of peace," in light of the fact that they have "one Lord, one faith, one baptism, [and] one God and Father of all." Baptism is about God, then about the church, and then about you. Likewise, the Lord's Supper teaches that we are "one body" and "one bread" in the Lord, drinking in "one Spirit" (1 Cor. 10:17; 12:13). If you say that baptism is the badge of your profession of faith and that the Lord's Supper is only about your communion with Christ, then you must ask what Paul might say to you. Don't the sacraments fundamental say, "It's not about you"? Other examples like these abound in the New Testament. Don't we see the covenant of grace behind texts like these, stressing the saving work of the triune God, and pressing the unity of the church through covenant signs? You need to get in line with

God's plan for the church instead of making covenant and church all about you.

The covenantal context of the church and its sacraments should make many things horribly unthinkable and other things indescribably great. Treating baptism primarily as a personal profession of faith should be unthinkable; regarding it as a sign of God's covenant promises to the church is great beyond measure. Taking the Lord's Supper in private, or making it exclusive to a bride and groom at a wedding, should repel us; observing it as a sign of Christ's union with believers and our union with Christ and his church should attract us. We should never want to receive baptism or the Lord's Supper alone. While the church, and the covenant on which it is founded, includes us, it is not primarily about us.

How many disputes in the church would be resolved if believers started thinking that the covenant and its signs are first about God, then others, and then themselves? In this light, arguments over what color the new carpet should be, which hymnal to buy, whether we find someone in the congregation offensive, and whether worship services interfere with Little League games no longer seem very important. Covenant and church go together, and what God has joined together, let no man put asunder.

## How Does Covenant Theology Teach Us to Live in the Family?

Human life usually begins in families. Whether families are stable or unstable, helpful or harmful, family connections shape who we are. Children look like their parents, whether or not they want to. Though parents and spouses cannot, and should not try to, make their children and spouses do and think whatever they want, family life inevitably shapes the speech, mannerisms, habits, and lives of everyone in the household. The covenant of grace affects people in a family even more profoundly because God not only sets the tone for the household but also promises to bring his influences into the hearts of family members in a way that no parent or spouse can do or try to do.

Covenant theology is a blessing because God brings families into covenant with himself, affecting families profoundly. In the covenant of works, Adam ruined his family. Through the covenant of redemption, Christ redeemed his family (1 Cor. 15:22), and the Spirit calls God's children home in the covenant of grace. God separated the seed of the woman from the seed of the serpent from Genesis 3:15 onward, dividing the nations by families. Being Abraham's God and the God of his children after him, God brought Abraham's family into the church through circumcision as a covenant sign (Gen. 17:1–12). The truth that God has put his word and Spirit in the mouths and hearts of believers, their children, and their children's children is one of the greatest encouragements to families under the new covenant (Isa. 59:21). God is our God and the God of our children, we are his people, and he dwells among us. Blessing families stands at the core of many of the most glorious promises of the covenant of grace. More than this, God's covenant with families should create a gospel-driven pattern for family life.

What does covenant theology mean for Christian families today? Though this is a broad topic with wide implications for how we live in our homes, marriage and children illustrate the point. The covenant of grace conveys the gospel to believing families, and how we live in marriage and with our children says a great deal about how we understand the gospel. For example, Paul did not merely tell husbands that they need to stop being selfish and mistreating their wives and start loving them. He said that husbands should love their wives "as Christ loved the church and gave himself up for her" (Eph. 5:25). As Christ "sanctif[ied]" and "cleansed" the church "by the washing of water with the word" (5:26), so husbands should imitate Christ's fulfillment of the covenant of redemption in loving their wives. Husbands should neither be selfish nor hate their wives; they should nourish and cherish them precisely because this reflects Christ's relationship with his church (5:29). Paul was so caught up in Christ's covenant work of saving his church that this overtook his discussion of marriage, though he concluded that his application was still relevant to married couples (5:32–33). Christ's covenant faithfulness to his church determines what a solid Christian husband should look like.

What should this look like concretely? Like Christ, husbands must deny themselves in loving service to their wives, letting Christ's covenant faithfulness set the tone in the home. Good Christology, or teaching about Christ, and good Trinitarian theology, comes before being a good Christian husband.[1] Husbands are in Christ, and Christ died for and sanctifies the church. This means that husbands will be more ready to listen to their wives than to speak. It means that they will lead through self-sacrifice rather than by demanding submission. Husbands will repent of harsh words and help with dishes and children instead of sitting in front of the television after a hard day's work. Every time I have asked men doing such things if they are reading their Bibles and praying consistently, they answer no. They put themselves first, over their wives and children, because they put God last. We could add examples for wives, but painting a general picture is what matters here.

The covenant presses Christ-centered perseverance through hardships in marriage as well. People with difficult marriages, even those

---

1   For an excellent Trinitarian and Christological approach to marriage, see John Piper, *This Momentary Marriage: A Parable of Permanence* (Wheaton, IL: Crossway, 2012).

married to unconverted spouses, will focus more on seeking Christ for his own sake in their marriages than desperately seeking to change spouses and circumstances, which are out of their control. Focusing on our circumstances leads to selfishness and anger; focusing on Christ and covenant leads to self-denial and humility. Such examples, and many more like them, are ways of putting God first, then the church, and then ourselves. The covenant is about the gospel of God, and how we live in marriage says volumes about our relationship to the God of the gospel.

The same things are true in relation to our children, who are God's children more than ours (Ezek. 16:21). God was God to Abraham, to his children after him, and to outsiders willing to join the church in the Old Testament. Abraham's promises still belong to us, to our children, and to as many as are afar off whom the Lord our God will call (Acts 2:38). The "blessing of Abraham" has come to the nations in Christ (Gal. 3:14). Baptizing households in the New Testament (Acts 16:15, 33; 1 Cor. 1:16), God brings salvation to the households of Abraham's believing sons (Luke 19:9). As noted in a previous chapter, God's covenant promises are one reason why most of the Christian church throughout its history has baptized the children of believers. I won't say much here about how we should view baptized covenant children but will focus instead on how the covenant transforms parenting. It is enough to say that God puts children in the church through baptism because they are in the covenant of grace through promises. They need to be born again and believe in Christ to take ownership of the covenant with God as their Father, and we need to teach them these facts. Children are not born again because they are born in Christian families, but the covenant of grace brings promises that God will ordinarily circumcise their hearts, putting his word and Spirit in them. Our children do not have fewer privileges and promises than Abraham's children did but better promises and blessings under a better covenant. We need to encourage our children to make these covenant promises their own.

The covenant of grace is a model for both Christian children and parents. Children need to obey their parents "in the Lord" because he is their Lord, because he has commanded it, and because he promises to bless them (Eph. 6:1–3). Fathers are obligated to rear their children in "the discipline and instruction of the Lord" (6:4) because God gives covenant promises to children and parents, requiring covenant obligations from both. We cannot control our children's hearts, and we cannot make them believers, both of which are the Holy Spirit's work. What we can do is bring them to the means of grace, where they can meet Christ, and teach them to expect God's work in their lives through his covenant faithfulness. In other words, we teach them to live by faith in the Son of God even as we do (Gal. 2:20). Teaching them how to live in utter dependence on Christ is more important than pressing for a moment of conversion.

As was the case with husbands and wives, this should make parents more ready to serve and to listen than to demand and to speak. Certainly, parents reflect Christ in their authority and teaching roles, and children need to obey them and learn from them, but parents should trust in God's covenant promises to them and to their children more than in their own parenting methods, repenting and asking their children for forgiveness when they do wrong.[2]

The gospel covenant directs gospel parenting even further. On the one hand, God requires first-time obedience from us, not letting

2  For a treatment of precisely the question in view here, see Joel R. Beeke, *Parenting by God's Promises: How to Raise Children in the Covenant of Grace* (Orlando: Reformation Trust, 2011).

us go our own way and hardening our hearts in sin. Letting people, whether adults or children, get away with sin without consequences and calling it grace is a sad commentary on our view of the covenant of grace. The grace of God that brings salvation teaches us "to renounce ungodliness and worldly passions, and to live self-controlled, upright, and godly lives in the present age" as we look to Christ's return (Titus 2:11–14). Christian parents, while being cautious not to require too much of their children, should require first-time obedience from their children because that is what our covenant God requires of us. On the other hand, God forgives our sins freely and unreservedly, not holding a grudge against us or calling up our past sins. So parents should forgive their children freely and move on quickly when they repent. Likewise, they should model such repentance toward their children when they sin against their children.

Lastly, as worship lies at the heart of the covenant of grace, so parents should lead their children in family worship. Simply put, this means setting apart time to worship God as a family. Simply practiced, we should set apart a brief time every day to read the Bible, pray, and sing together. What better way to show that we are in covenant with God than gathering daily to pray to the triune God, to praise him, and to read and listen to his word? Remember, however, that worship is for families and not only for children. Married couples without children, or without children in the home, are still families in covenant with God who should express covenant blessings through worshiping God together. To be profitable, family worship should be simple, short, regular, and predictable. Better to do a little bit daily and consistently than to quit because of unrealistic expectations.[3]

3  For help with family worship, see Joel R. Beeke, *Family Worship* (Grand Rapids, MI: Reformation Heritage Books, 2009).

## How Does Covenant Theology Teach
## Individual Christians How to Live?

Individuals come last in the covenant, but they are not left out. Covenant theology answers life's biggest questions: who God is, who we are, what our problem is, what God has done about it, and how we come to know him. Showing us not only who God is but also who he is to us, the covenant of grace brings us into fellowship with God, through his Son, and by his Spirit. The covenant of works shows why we needed to be saved from our sins, the covenant of redemption shows us what Christ did to redeem us, and the covenant of grace shows us how we come to experience salvation. Covenant theology means that we are not our own. Having been bought with a price (1 Cor. 6:20), we live life by faith in the Son of God, who loved us and gave himself for us (Gal. 2:20). Whether we eat or drink, work or play, sleep or awake, are married or single, are rich or poor, are male or female, are adult or child, we respond to the covenant properly by using all we have and by doing all that we do to the glory of God (1 Cor. 10:31). We serve God with body and soul, even in mundane day-to-day life, as we look to the resurrection and everlasting life. Covenant faithfulness to God consists largely in learning to do the right things, in the right ways, and at the right times, including things like work, sleep, and play.

Covenant blessings to individuals should, among other things, produce daily Bible reading and prayer, self-denial, self-control, the fruit of the Spirit, Sabbath keeping, loving public worship and prayer meetings, enjoying fellowship with God's people, and service to the church. Just as we must be born of the Spirit and believe in Christ to repent and come to the Father, so we walk by the Spirit, seeking everything we need from Christ, so that we might honor God with our lives. This is both what the covenant of grace demands and what it promises.

So to summarize what we have discovered, covenant theology is a blessing because it shows us the breathtaking unity of Scripture, leads us to know the triune God, and teaches us how to live in the church, in the family, and as individuals. These are also the basics of covenant theology, revolving as they do around the Son, the seed, and the sacraments. I pray that our discussions so far are enough to get you started in seeing and living in the blessings of covenant theology, making you hunger and thirst for more. The questions in the next section offer a little bit more, and the recommended resources show you where you can find more.

## Questions

1. How should covenant theology make the church a priority in our lives? Are there areas in our lives in which we need to prioritize the church more than we do?

2. Why does the covenant lead us to put Christ first in marriage? How can the covenant of grace transform difficult marriages into blessed ones?

3. For the unmarried, how can the Christ-focused nature of the covenant of grace shape your priorities in praying over a potential spouse?

4. In what ways should the gospel shape the relationship between parents and children? Why does parenting reflect our understanding of the covenant of grace?

5. How can you exercise self-denial in prioritizing worship, the church, and fellow believers?

# Questions and Answers
# about Covenant Theology

MOST BIBLE DOCTRINES invite lots of questions. The more widely these questions reach into every page of Scripture, the broader their implications are. Below are some questions about covenant theology that you may have thought of or encountered; others you might not have heard before, but others are asking them. The answers are brief and to the point, and resources for fuller answers are provided in the recommended reading section at the end of the book.

In lieu of additional study questions, I close each segment with a single question for reflection. Study groups can take a few of the questions below at a time, using the concluding questions to promote further discussion.

### What Are Some Other Ways of Defining Covenants?

Summarizing many older authors, I define *covenant* as a contract or agreement with parties, promises, conditions, and sanctions. Many people today do not like this definition because they think that it either sounds too cold and contractual or demeans God, putting him on the same level as his creatures. Alternatives include general ideas like relationship, promise, or oath, and specific ideas like a "bond in blood sovereignly administered."[1] While contract or agreement may be imperfect, the problem is that broader and narrower definitions include either too little or too much biblical material. While promises and oaths remain central to covenants, people make promises or take oaths in the Bible without making covenants, such as Joshua putting Achan under oath to confess his sin (Josh. 7:19). We have already seen that David and Jonathan made a covenant without a bond in blood, or sacrifice.

As far as God covenanting or contracting with human beings, we also need to remember that the Bible does not pit law against love. God's law, and God's covenant contracts, demand loving faith and obedience. Covenants as contracts or agreements does not demean God because God is free to enter covenants or not do so. In this sense, the fact that God would make any covenant, whether of works or grace, is an act of unspeakable condescension, love, and even grace.

Why does our definition of *covenant* matter?

## What Key Words Help Us Find Covenants in Scripture, Even Where the Term *Covenant* Is Not in the Text?

In addition to identifying the parts of a covenant, or key names like Abraham and David, the Hebrew Bible particularly uses *emet* and especially *chesed* as key covenantal terms. Defining these terms is hard, due to their wide meaning, but they usually appear in our English Bibles as "truth" or "faithfulness" and "mercy" or "steadfast love." God's revelation of his "name" to Moses in Exodus 34:5–7 stresses

---

1    O. Palmer Robertson, *The Christ of the Covenants* (Phillipsburg, NJ: Presbyterian and Reformed Publishing, 1980), 4.

that he abounds in *chesed* and *emet* ("steadfast love and faithfulness," 34:6) and that he keeps his *chesed* for thousands (34:7). While God's covenant "steadfast love" endures forever (Ps. 136), the "love" of the church is, unfortunately, sometimes "like a morning cloud, / like the dew that goes early away" (Hos. 6:4). God's anger lasts a moment, but his *chesed* ("favor") endures for life (Ps. 30:5). In the well-known words of Psalm 23, his goodness and *chesed* ("mercy") follow us all the days of our lives (Ps. 23:6).

We usually see allusions to the covenant in our English Bibles when God uses terms like "mercy and truth" in the NKJV or "steadfast love" and "faithfulness" in the ESV, especially together. I recommend reading the ESV for the Psalms in particular because it consistently translates *chesed* as "steadfast love" and *emet* as faithfulness, making it easier for English readers to identify key covenant terms and ideas.

Psalm 25 is a good example applying these terms. There the psalmist pleads with God to remember his *emet* and *chesed* ("mercy" and "steadfast love" in the ESV). Making explicit reference to the covenant, 25:10 adds that all of God's ways are *chesed* and *emet* ("steadfast love and faithfulness") to those who keep his covenant. Often, the Psalms also translate *chesedim* as "saints," showing that believers reflect God's covenant faithfulness, or "steadfast love" with their own (Ps. 31:23; 31:24 in Hebrew). Psalm 52, in which David prays against Doeg's betrayal, brings these terms together. The psalm begins with a meditation on God's *chesed* (52:1) and ends with trust in God's *chesed* (52:8) and praises the Lord in the presence of "the godly" (*chasideka*, 52:9). Psalm 89, celebrating God's covenant with David, uses *chesed*, *emet*, *chesedim*, and *covenant* together throughout the Psalm.

Given this Old Testament covenant background, it is hard to miss John's allusion to God's *chesed* and *emet* when he describes the only begotten of the Father as coming "full of grace and truth" (John 1:14) and of Christ bringing "grace and truth" (1:17). Keeping in mind what we learned about God's *chesed* and *emet* from the Old Testament makes reading these verses even more meaningful and exciting. Jesus embodied and fulfilled God's covenant faithfulness, spreading the covenant to all nations.

Can you think of other passages where you might find either *emet* or *chesed*, or both together?

## How Is Marriage a Covenant?

Malachi 2:14–16 is the only explicit reference in Scripture to marriage as a covenant, which illustrates the usefulness of defining the term "covenant" broadly. The prophet assumed that his hearers took it for granted that marriage was covenantal. Illustrating that not all relationships are covenantal, but covenants refer to special relationships, marriage illustrates the nature of covenants, in their broadest sense, and covenant explains the nature of the marital relationship.

First, a covenant is present where its parts are present, even if the Bible does not always use the word. Husband and wife are covenant parties, making promises to God and each other by oath, in order to fulfill conditions of covenant faithfulness, with implied sanctions on breaking the marriage covenant. No sacrifices or sacraments attach to marriage since the oath is prominent in marriage without outward sensible signs and seals. We use rings in our culture, but these are, strictly speaking, not so much covenant signs as a social custom. Marriage is not a sacrament, even though it points to Christ's relation to his church, because it is a contracted relationship rather than an outward sensible sign.

Second, the covenantal oath constitutes marriage, making the two one flesh. The sexual union of husband and wife appears in this context, but a couple is married as soon as they take their vows, or oaths. Jesus permitted divorce for sexual infidelity (Matt. 19:9) because such actions break the marriage covenant. So does willful and irremediable physical desertion (1 Cor. 7:15). While divorce today often is due to fault on both sides, the Bible stresses freedom to remarry on the side of the one who kept and did not break the essential bond of the marriage covenant.

How does marriage reveal the place of oaths in covenants?

## Can Someone Still Hold to the Gospel without Covenant Theology?

Yes, though not as clearly as they would with covenant theology. Many people, for example, deny that God made a covenant with Adam, but they still believe that we are dead in Adam and need to be made alive in Christ in light of Romans 5:12–21. What they are missing is the ability to explain the reasons behind the parallels and contrasts that Paul drew between Adam and Christ. Holding to the gospel without a clear covenant theology is like taking a picture before letting the camera focus fully. The picture remains the same, but it is not as clear as it could have been and should have been if we took the time to focus the lens.

How does covenant theology help explain the parallels between Adam and Christ?

## Is Covenant Theology a New View in History?

No and yes. Just like the idea of covenant is in the Bible, even when the term does not always appear, so it has been in church history. For example, the early church, countering Judaism initially, was concerned to show the unity of the Old and New Testaments. Cyril of Jerusalem (313–386) argued in his catechetical lectures for the unity of God and the gospel in the Old and New Testaments against the Manicheans, who denied both. Augustine (354–430) devoted books 16–18 of his *City of God*, among other places, to demonstrating the unity of the church throughout the ages in contrast to the world. Such authors used covenant ideas, and covenant language now and then, to describe the unity of the Bible's message, though the term was not prominent in their writings. Thomas Aquinas (1225–1274) liked to refer to friendship with God in places where Reformed authors would usually insert covenant theology. The substance of covenant theology is not new in church history, though the terms are not always present.

However, covenant theology developed most explicitly in Reformation and post-Reformation Reformed theology. Instead of merely treating original sin, with occasional vague references to a covenant between God and Adam, Reformed authors began to refer to a covenant of works, at least from the late sixteenth century onward. The covenant of grace and the unity of the Old and New Testaments were consistent themes in Reformed theology from the beginning, just as they were in the early and medieval church. Yet the covenant of redemption, or covenant of the mediator, became explicit around the 1640s and after. Even in this case, all the ideas of the covenant of redemption appeared in early church, medieval, and earlier Reformed authors, especially in relation to the doctrine of election.

Covenant theology was new in the sense of its organization and terminology, but it was not really new in terms of its ideas. More careful study of Scripture during and after the Reformation led to using a biblical term like "covenant" more naturally and prevalently to teach and clarify ideas that the church always held to in some form.

In what ways can the idea of covenant be more important than the presence of the term?

## Why Is Covenant Theology Usually Attached to Reformed Theology?

This is a good question in light of how often the term "covenant" appears in the Bible. Conservative Jewish theology always has taught, and likely will continue to teach, some form of covenant theology because the term forces itself on anyone reading the Hebrew Bible. Reformed theology picks up the same trends in Scripture, with a fuller picture completed in the New Testament.

Yet even Lutheran and Roman Catholic theologians have taught covenant theologies over the ages, though not with the same prominence that Reformed churches have devoted to the theme. This is particularly true in relation to biblical studies, where people from every theological tradition claiming to be Christian need to wrestle with the language of the Bible itself. In short, everyone who reads and believes the Bible has a covenant theology. The question is how much importance they attach to covenant ideas. Reformed theology stands out by emphasizing covenant as a key part of understanding Scripture and the gospel.

Why does everyone taking the Bible seriously end up with a covenant theology?

## What Is the Main Difference between Covenant Theology and Other Alternatives?

There are many alternatives to covenant theology, including dispensational theology, new covenant theology, and liberal theology. Liberal theology tends to dismiss parts of the Bible as uninspired and often denies a unified message throughout its books. Risking oversimplifi-cation, the general marker of the first two alternatives lies in the rela-tionship between Israel and the church. Are Israel and the church two peoples of God with two distinct destinies in the future, one earthly and one heavenly (especially in the case of dispensationalism)? Or is Israel the church under the old covenant, flowing seamlessly into the new covenant church, like one olive tree sharing Jewish and Gentile branches (Rom. 11:24)? The text I cite here shows my hand. Being the "Israel of God" (Gal. 6:16), the new covenant church does not replace Israel, but Gentiles are grafted into the true Israel, which is one church spanning all ages and places of the world. Liberal theology goes fur-ther, teaching that there may be as many covenant theologies as there are authors of the Bible. After all, if God is not the primary author of the Bible, then why look for a theme uniting its books?

The Lutheran distinction between the law and the gospel stands out as a time-tested alternative to covenant theology as well. Luther and post-Reformation Lutheran theologians tended to divide law and gospel in terms of works versus grace. Thus, the law presents threats and conditions, while the gospel brings unconditional promises. This meant that any part of Scripture containing commands and threats was law and that any unconditional promises were gospel, resulting in a method of reading two unifying themes in parallel throughout the whole Bible, rather than one unifying covenant of grace.

Reformed theology picked up law/gospel language and used it freely, but Reformed authors gradually redefined law and gospel in terms of the covenants of works and of grace. What Lutheran and Reformed theology have in common in using law/gospel terminology is that both believe that we are justified by faith alone in Christ apart from the works of the law (Rom. 3:28). However, Reformed theology has not tended to divide Scripture into law and gospel with conditions and sanctions in one category and unconditional promises in the other. All covenants include promises, conditions, and sanctions, including the covenants of works and of grace. Though Reformed authors believed that some parts of Scripture under the covenant of grace alluded to the covenant of works, the covenants of works and of grace were primarily historical eras in biblical history with lasting effects, rather than a hermeneutical key divided according to conditions and promises.

How can alternatives to covenant theology affect our understanding of the Bible?

## Does Covenant Theology Demand a Particular Millennial Viewpoint?

It is unfortunate that the so-called millennium has diverted so much of the church's attention in the past one hundred fifty years. Appearing in only one difficult-to-interpret passage of Scripture (Rev. 20:1–6), the millennium has hijacked modern eschatology, or the study of the last things.

From the beginning of the Christian church, eschatology focused on the "beatific vision," or blessed sight of the triune God in heaven (1 John 3:1–2). Pastors thought of the most pressing eschatological questions as death, judgment, heaven, and hell since they ministered to people who needed to prepare to die and meet Christ. The resurrection is a focal point, drawing a circle around these issues, because the resurrection is tied to the final fulfillment of the covenant of grace for believers. Today, however, if someone asks what one believes about eschatology, they usually mean, "What is your view of the millennium?" The Bible mentions the millennium, so we should not ignore it, but the tendency among many people to let a few verses direct how they read everything else in the Bible, instead of understanding those obscure verses in light of the rest of Scripture, is unhealthy and inappropriate. Placing the beatific vision back at the center of Christian eschatology is much wiser and more profitable.[2]

What about covenant theology and the millennium? Generally, millennial questions focus on whether Christ's thousand-year reign begins before or after his second coming. If the millennium starts before his second coming, then this is postmillennialism, since Christ returns "post" the millennium. However, if Christ returns prior to the millennium, then we call this premillennialism. The result is that there are ultimately only two millennial views in relation to the order of Christ's return, post and pre.

What about the view known as "amillennialism"? Amillennialism means that the thousand years in Revelation 20 are not a literal millennium but a figurative number for a long time. In this sense, postmillennialists can be amillennialists, believing that Christ reigns now on earth, encompassing the entire time between his first and second comings. I suppose that premillennialists could be amillennialist too, though most of the time this group expects a more or less literal thousand-year reign after Christ's second coming, followed by rebellion and a final judgment.

Many times, however, pre- and amillennial views describe how optimistic one is about the spread of the gospel in the present age. Amillennialists can lean toward very pessimistic views of decline on the one side, and on the other very optimistic views of the spread of the gospel, though they are somewhat agnostic about the details.

2  See Michael Allen, *Grounded in Heaven: Recentering Christian Hope and Life on God* (Grand Rapids, MI: Eerdmans, 2018).

Postmillennialists can likewise range toward the middle of the spectrum, still allowing room for persecution and opposition to an expanding church, or toward the extreme of speaking as though almost everyone in the world will profess faith in Christ before he returns.

All three millennial views are potentially compatible with covenant theology. So long as people believe in one covenant of grace and essentially one church in the old and new covenants, then they can hold to Reformed covenant theology. Whether premillennialism fits the confessional documents of many Reformed churches regarding the timing of Christ's return is another question, which each church needs to work out. Dispensational premillennialism,[3] however, is incompatible with covenant theology because it divides Israel and the church in a way that displaces the unity of the covenant of grace, largely relegating the old covenant to Israel and the new covenant to the church. In every case, however, millennial views should never displace our hope in the resurrection of the dead at Christ's return.

Why should the millennium be less prominent than it often is in studies of the last things?

## Are the Covenants of Redemption and Grace Really Distinct Covenants?

Many Reformed authors today collapse the covenant of redemption into the covenant of grace. Rather than two distinct covenants regarding the salvation of the elect, one eternal and one in time, the idea is that the covenant of grace has eternal and temporal aspects. Those adopting this view often believe that it is simpler to teach one

3 The main feature of all forms of dispensationalism is that proponents view Israel and the church as two peoples of God with two distinct destinies.

covenant of grace that includes everything that we need to say about redemption planned, accomplished, and applied than it is to treat the covenant of redemption as a distinct covenant between the Father and the Son. Others have gone further, rejecting the covenant of redemption because they believe that a covenant among the persons of the Trinity denies the single divine will.

At least two factors illustrate why it is better to distinguish the covenant of redemption from the covenant of grace. First, the parties, promises, conditions, and sanctions differ in both covenants. The Father promised things to the Son that would be blasphemous for us to claim, such as the ability to give the Holy Spirit to the nations and receive the name above every name before which all in heaven and earth will bow. The Son's conditions are suffering and obedience in the place of sinners, which only a God-man could fulfill. Who could bear his sanctions, and whose suffering can measure up to his? God's promises to us likewise cannot apply to Christ since, for example, God promises to change our hearts and forgive our sins. Faith is the condition through which we receive Christ, and covenant sanctions fall on those who turn their backs on Christ, even though they never really belonged to him (1 John 2:19). Collapsing the eternal covenant of redemption into the historical covenant of grace makes both covenants less intelligible because it jumbles together incompatible promises, conditions, and sanctions. I have explained already why the covenant of redemption does not imply three wills in God. God has one will, exercised from the Father, through the Son, by the Spirit.

Second, distinguishing the covenants of redemption and grace guards the gospel against both legalism and antinomianism. Legalism here means seeking to earn God's favor by obedience or law keeping.

Antinomianism means that the grace of the gospel makes law keeping irrelevant, if not irreverent. The covenant of redemption rules out legalism by resting the gospel on the gracious foundation of Christ's work as mediator; it is unconditional for the elect. However, the covenant of grace is conditioned on faith in Christ, which the Spirit gives us because of Christ's work in the covenant of redemption. This faith works by loving obedience, leaving no room for antinomianism. Collapsing the covenants of redemption and grace has the disadvantage of either denying any conditions in the gospel covenant, leaving the place of faith and repentance ambiguous, or neglecting the gospel's unconditional foundations.

While good theologians hold to both views, the older majority Reformed view of one eternal covenant and two historical ones (works and grace) seems to fit the Bible and theology best. To be clear, this is not so much a three-covenant view as it is the idea that an eternal covenant stands behind everything God does in time, with a first and second covenant in human history.

What are the advantages of distinguishing the covenants of redemption and of grace?

## Is the Covenant of Grace Conditional or Unconditional?

This question arises from the preceding one. Collapsing the covenants of redemption and grace into a single covenant tends to place all covenant conditions on Christ, raising the question of whether any conditions remain for the elect. I imply throughout the material above that our participation in the covenant of grace is conditioned on faith, which Christ purchased for us and the Spirit gives us by virtue of the covenant of redemption. Calling the covenant of grace "the second covenant," Westminster Larger Catechism 32 reflects this viewpoint:

The grace of God is manifested in the second covenant, in that he freely provideth and offereth to sinners a Mediator, and life and salvation by him; and requiring faith as the condition to interest them in him, promiseth and giveth his Holy Spirit to all his elect, to work in them that faith, with all other saving graces; and to enable them unto all holy obedience, as the evidence of the truth of their faith and thankfulness to God, and as the way which he hath appointed them to salvation.[4]

If the covenant of grace brings Christ to believers, then faith in Christ is the condition of receiving covenant blessings. Obedience is not a condition of the covenant because we receive Christ by faith and not by works. Yet the Holy Spirit produces other saving graces in us through union with Christ by faith, enabling us to walk in covenant faithfulness on the path to final salvation in heaven. The covenant of grace is conditioned on faith, while faith evidences itself through works.

Assuming saving faith, Psalms 111–112 illustrate the reciprocal nature of the covenant of grace. Both Psalms are acrostics, each line beginning with a sequential letter of the Hebrew alphabet to help people memorize them. Reflecting each other, Psalm 111 is about the righteous God and Psalm 112 is about his righteous people, with "his righteousness endures forever" being the key phrase in both cases (Pss. 111:3; 112:3, 9). God remembers his covenant with his people (111:5), establishing it forever (111:9). In turn, God's covenant faithfulness in Psalm 111 finds reflection in the character of his righteous people in Psalm 112. The covenant of grace is reciprocal in

4  WLC q. 32 (*CCC* 345).

that God's covenant faithfulness both demands and creates covenant faithfulness in his people.

While faith is the condition of uniting us to Christ and entering the covenant of grace, faith in Christ leads to lives of covenant faithfulness. Christ secures our faith and our faithfulness by the covenant of redemption, and the Spirit enables us to receive Christ and live faithfully in the covenant of grace.

Why is faith the condition of the covenant of grace, and why is this important?

### How Does Covenant Theology Relate to the Canon of Scripture?

Covenants as a unifying theme in Scripture raises a practical question about which books are included in Scripture. The Jewish church accepted only those books that are also found in Protestant Bibles today, excluding additions like Susannah, Bel and the Dragon, 1 and 2 Second Maccabees, and others. Some of our Roman Catholic friends have asked why, if we make so much out of the Bible, we do not include all the books they have in their Bibles.

Covenant theology gives a partial answer to this question. Some general considerations are in order first.[5] In the early church, Augustine of Hippo questioned some of the so-called apocryphal books. In one place in *City of God*, he ruled some of them out because of their uncertain origin and content, concluding that "no reliance is placed on them; and this is particularly true of those in which statements are found that actually contradict the reliable evidence of the canonical

---

5  For a couple of recent books on this topic, see Michael J. Kruger, *Canon Revisited: Establishing the Origins and Authority of the New Testament Books* (Wheaton, IL: Crossway, 2012); Kruger, *The Question of Canon: Challenging the Status Quo in the New Testament Debate* (Nottingham, UK: Apollos, 2018).

books, so that it is immediately apparent that they are not authentic."[6]
Earlier in *City of God*, he argued that the Apocrypha had obscure
origins and authorship and that they were not preserved from antiq-
uity in the Jewish Church. Noting that we can still learn from them
because they contain many true things, he added, "All these have been
excluded from canonical authority as a result of careful examination,
and are classed as Apocrypha."[7] Though Augustine primarily had the
so-called Prophecy of Enoch directly in view, his arguments became
relevant later in Reformed theology.[8]

The Reformed theologian Francis Turretin (1623–1687) summarized four reasons for rejecting apocryphal books: God did not direct
the Jewish church to recognize them, Christ and the apostles did not
quote them as authoritative, the Christian church rejected them for
four hundred years, and prophets did not write them (nor are they
in Hebrew).[9] He included Augustine's rule of contradicting canonical books within this list. This at least explains why Protestants and
Jews include fewer books in their Bibles than Roman Catholics and
Eastern Orthodox do.

How does this question relate to covenant theology? Augustine's
rule is relevant here. If the Bible is a unified message about God's covenant with his people, then what are these books about, and do they
contradict its message? Susannah illustrates the disjunction between

6  Augustine, *City of God*, trans. Henry Bettenson (London: Penguin, 1984), bk. 18,
   par. 38 (813).
7  Augustine, *City of God*, bk. 15, par. 23 (641).
8  Chap. 1 of the Second Helvetic Confession, an early and enduring Reformed confession, cites *City of God*, bk. 18, par. 38 (812–13), against including apocryphal
   books.
9  Francis Turretin, *Institutes of Elenctic Theology*, ed. James T. Dennison, trans. George
   Musgrave Giger (Phillipsburg, NJ: P&R, 1992), 102–3.

the Apocrypha and God's covenant story, which is listed as Daniel 13 in the Apocrypha. Daniel is about establishing God's kingdom over all the nations of the earth. Remembering his covenant with his people to dwell with them and be their God, God promised he would establish an eternal kingdom compassing all the kingdoms of the earth (Dan. 2), he showed that his dominance over Nebuchadnezzar of Babylon (Dan. 2–4), he showed that the Ancient of Days would make the Son of Man king of this kingdom (Dan. 7), and he showed that the Messiah would fulfill prophesy and bring an end to sacrifices (Dan. 9). Daniel prayed toward the temple three times a day (Dan. 6), even under threats, because he remembered Solomon's temple prayer that God would remember his people when they prayed toward the place of his covenant presence (1 Kings 8). Whether Daniel faced the lion's den or his friends found themselves in the fiery furnace, God's kingdom resting on his covenant is the grand theme of the book. This fits God's unified covenantal message in other books by stressing the Son, his seed, his relationship to the nations, and his covenant presence.

What about Susannah? This "book" is about a young woman who is assaulted by two old men who want to sleep with her. When she refuses, they act as two false witnesses, accusing her of immorality and demanding that she be burned. Since she had no other witnesses beyond God, Daniel intervenes, telling the crowd what really happened, resulting in the deaths of Susannah's accusers. A looming question is, What does this have to do with the grand theme of the book of Daniel, let alone the Bible?" The answer is that this story seems jarringly out of place. Where is the covenant? Where is God's presence with his people and the call to repentance as the people return from exile and prepare for the Messiah's coming? Borrowing from Augustine and Turretin, we may say that this story contradicts other parts of Scripture, not so much because it teaches false doctrine or ethics but because it has nothing to do with the Bible's story.

By contrast, God may be muted in the background in a book like Esther, but readers can still see God's preservation of his people for the sake of his covenant. Yet Daniel and the rest of the Old Testament is far more explicit than this about fitting into God's covenantal story. Susannah seems random, leaving readers who have learned to follow God's storyline scratching their heads as to how it relates to anything else.

How does covenant theology shape the canon of Scripture?

## Is There a Difference between Covenant and Testament?

Westminster Confession of Faith 7.4 says, "This covenant of grace is frequently set forth in Scripture by the name of a testament, in reference to the death of Jesus Christ the Testator, and to the everlasting inheritance, with all things belonging to it, therein bequeathed."[10] Hebrews 9:15–17 is the backdrop, in which the KJV translates the Greek word for covenant as "testament" in 9:15 (and 9:18) but "testament" and "Testator" in between. This raises a substantial question requiring a more substantial answer than I can give here, but here are a few seed thoughts:

First, "testament" in Westminster Confession 7.4 is not about the translation of one or a few texts, but it includes a general idea that pervades the covenant of grace. While some argue that the Westminster Assembly merely referred to the frequent occurrence of testament instead of covenant in the KJV, this is wrong. The assembly believed that the covenant of grace carried a testamentary idea, which was "frequently" the prominent idea of the covenant of grace.

---

10  WCF 7.4 (*CCC* 196).

Second, a testament referred to a special kind of covenant. The ESV picks up the idea by translating the covenantal language in Hebrews 9:15–17 as "will." When someone makes a will, they determine who receives their inheritance after they die. The Westminster Confession, appealing to the argument of Hebrews 9:15–17, is saying that the covenant of grace is a testamentary covenant. The idea is that all testaments are covenants, but not all covenants are testaments. All covenants are contracts or agreements between two or more parties, but some covenants emphasize God's sovereign promise and gift. In other words, older authors used the language of a last will and testament to emphasize that God rooted every promise of the covenant of grace in Christ's death.

Instead of creating a narrow definition of *covenant* that applied to the covenant of grace alone, the Westminster divines drew from a narrower existing category of covenant to say what they needed to say about the covenant of grace. This means that the testamentary idea is present whenever the Scriptures stress the gracious character of the gospel covenant as rooted in Christ's death. Hebrews 9:15–17 merely explains how and why this is the case. When the KJV called the Lord's Supper Christ's "blood of the new testament" (Matt. 26:28), this was a theological statement rather than a stylistic variation in translation. The testament in Christ's death leads to our hope of resurrection in his life.

What aspects of the covenant of grace does "testament" direct our attention to?

## How Does the Covenant Relate to the Church and to Apostasy?

As many have said, the covenant is the charter and foundation of the church. *Covenant* and *church* are not synonymous, but the church mirrors and mimics the covenant. Christ built his church on the new covenant in his blood. People belong to the covenant before they belong to the church, which is why baptism solemnly admits into the church those who show that they belong under the administration of the covenant of grace, whether through birth into covenant families or professions of faith by those who had no prior connection to the church.

The church also tells us something about the covenant, since God administers the covenant in the church. Not all who are in the church are of the church. In the same way, not all who are in the covenant are of the covenant. There is a difference between the administration of the covenant of grace in the visible aspect of the church, and the essence of the covenant of grace in the invisible aspect of the church. There are not two covenants of grace here any more than there are two churches, but both covenant and church have aspects visible to God alone and aspects visible both to God and to people.

Apostasy, or abandoning one's profession of faith in Christ and membership in the church, is covenant breaking, further strengthening the link between church and covenant. This issue can become a huge can of worms. Suffice it to say that the Bible presents three categories of people, not two: believers, unbelievers, and apostates. Those who leave the church never truly belonged to her (1 John 2:19), and every born-again elect person can neither "totally nor finally" fall away from Christ.[11] Yet when people abandon their profession of God's covenant promises and are cut off from the fellowship of the church, they end up worse off than where they started (2 Pet. 2:20). The Bible uses strong language here. Such people trample the Son of

11  WCF 17.1 (*CCC* 210).

God underfoot, profane the blood of the "covenant" that sanctified them, and insult "the Spirit of grace" (Heb. 10:29). They deny "the Master who bought them" (2 Pet. 2:1). Hebrews and Peter do not use "sanctified" and "bought" here to refer to the Spirit and Christ's work in and for the elect. They refer to an external sanctification and "union" with Christ in the visible church under the administration of the covenant of grace.

Some people say that the contrast between the old covenant and the new is that covenant breaking is no longer possible. Everyone in the new covenant is also of the new covenant. Jeremiah 31:31–34 could make this sound plausible if read in isolation, but other texts like the ones cited above show that the distinction between covenant essence as well as administration and the ways in which the church reflects the covenant of grace continue in the new covenant.

How do the essence and administration of the covenant help us understand practical issues like apostasy in the church?

### How Does the Holy Spirit Relate to the Old and New Covenants?

In short, the Holy Spirit gave gifts and graces, both in the old and new covenants, but he gives more gifts and greater graces in the new. The main question is whether the Spirit indwelled saints under the old covenant, or whether his indwelling is peculiar to the new covenant.

I confess that I can't answer this question adequately. In John 3, Jesus assumed that Nicodemus should have understood the necessity of the new birth even under the old covenant, likely considering circumcision and some of the promises of Moses and the prophets. Yet indwelling is more than new birth. The Spirit's indwelling goes hand in hand with union with Christ, which flows from his finished work. This would seem to indicate that the Spirit changed hearts in the old covenant without dwelling within believers.

Yet from a Christian standpoint, we have difficulty grasping how God could communicate saving grace to believers without union with Christ through the indwelling Spirit. Though the Old Testament saints came to God, through Christ, by the Spirit, it appears likely that God applied the benefits of Christ's work in advance without explicit union with Christ and the indwelling of the Spirit. How this worked is likely beyond our ability to explain. We know that if the Spirit of him who raised Christ from the dead is in us, then God will also give life to our mortal bodies (Rom. 8:11). God will resurrect us in Christ, and he will raise the Old Testament saints. We should hope in these facts whether or not we can explain them adequately.

Why is the Spirit's indwelling in the Old Testament a difficult matter to explain?

## Why Is Our Communion with God in the New Covenant Greater Than Adam's in the Covenant of Works?

Related partially to the previous question, God dwelt with Adam, but not in Adam. Under the new covenant, the Spirit dwells in believers' hearts, and because he is inseparable from the Father and the Son, the Father and Son dwell in us too. More particularly, union with Christ means that everything Christ did, he did in our place. We share in his humiliation and exaltation. The Spirit who dwelt in him dwells in us. His death under sin's curse removes the curse and power of sin from us. God counts his righteous life to us. We live and will be raised through his resurrection. His place in heaven secures ours. God's covenant presence in us, which is distinctively and unmistakably Trinitarian, is better than God's covenant presence with Adam.

Yet there is more to say. Westminster Larger Catechism 39 tells us that one reason that the Son of God became man was "that he might advance our nature."[12] Our humanity in Christ advances above what it was in its created state. We are not merely renewed in God's image, but we bear the image better as the Spirit renews the image in us in Christ (Rom. 8:29). Hebrews 2:5–9, citing Psalm 8, argues that while God created man lower than the angels, he crowned him with glory and honor. Christ brought about this reality by becoming man, "made lower than the angels," but was then "crowned with glory and honor because of the suffering of death" (Heb. 2:9). As God, the Son is Lord of the angels, but as man, Christ became better than the angels by inheritance (Heb. 1:4). At the resurrection, we shall be greater than the angels, being conformed to the image of Christ's glorious body (Phil. 3:21). Just as we bore the image of the "man of dust," so shall we bear the image of the "man of heaven" (1 Cor. 15:49). Christ advances our human nature because we share in the exaltation of his glorified humanity, which surpasses both Adam and the angels. Our resurrection from the dead in union with Christ is thus the capstone of covenant blessings.

Explaining these glorious truths fully is beyond us. Through spiritual and internal fellowship with the triune God, we become "partakers" of the divine nature (2 Pet. 1:4) without becoming divine. While this far exceeds our comprehension, we will bless God eternally that he worked through Adam's sin and provided Jesus as our Savior, making our blessedness in Christ greater than if Adam had never fallen.

How should Christ's work of advancing our human nature excite our communion with God?

12  WLC q. 39 (*CCC* 347).

## Was There Grace in the Covenant of Works?

Yes, there was grace in the covenant of works, but in a manner radically different from the covenant of grace. The fact that God made a covenant with Adam at all and that the life promised was disproportionate to the obedience offered was gracious on God's part, in the sense of giving Adam more than he deserved by nature.

Excluding redemptive grace, however, God did not give Adam a mediator, and Adam did not need the Spirit to change his heart and renew his life. Adam still had to depend on God in faith and obedience, since a creature becomes a sinner as soon as he or she declares independence from God. This is why the Holy Spirit filled Christ's humanity with gifts and graces (e.g., Isa. 11:1–6), even though he was not a sinner and had no need of redemptive grace.

We could say that in the covenant of works, the terms were legal, but the promise was gracious; but in the covenant of grace, both the terms and the promises are gracious. The covenant of works graciously promised life for obedience, while the covenant of grace graciously supplies the Spirit to work faith, repentance, union with Christ, sanctification, and a host of other blessings that excel both the terms and the promise of the covenant of works. God also promises resurrection life in Christ, which outstrips anything Adam could have known without falling into sin. Of course, if someone objects to applying the term *grace* to the promise of the covenant of works, then this is fine, so long as that person affirms that the reward promised was disproportionate to the obedience offered. We should be more concerned with ideas than with words in this case.

Why is making a covenant with human beings always an act of grace on God's part?

## Did God "Republish" the Covenant of Works in the Mosaic Covenant?

Based on what I wrote earlier, the Mosaic covenant is an administration of the covenant of grace. It is the "legal administration" of the covenant of grace, but it is not a covenant of works. However, many people have seen traces of the covenant of works in the Mosaic covenant in commands like "do this and live" (see Lev. 18:5) and in covenant blessings and curses (e.g., Lev. 26; Deut. 28). Whether calling this a covenant of works or a conditional aspect of the Mosaic covenant keeping Israel in the land, some have argued that the Ten Commandments in particular contain a republication of the covenant of works. Two points may help think through the relationship between the Mosaic covenant and the covenant of works.

First, the same law that God used in the covenant of works is published in the Decalogue in the Mosaic covenant. However, the law reflects God's holy character before it serves as the terms of a covenant. God used the law as a covenant of works, but the covenant of works is not inherent in the law. This is the only reason why the law can serve as a rule for sanctification and godliness in the covenant of grace, which was its primary function under Moses.

Second, the law reminds us of the covenant of works without necessarily being given as a covenant of works. Christ took up the law as a covenant by virtue of the covenant of redemption to obey and suffer in the place of those who broke the covenant of works. How can anyone outside of Christ look at the Mosaic law and see anything less than condemnation through Adam under the covenant of works? Yet this does not mean that this was the primary reason why God gave the law to Moses. "Because God is the Lord, and our God, and Redeemer, therefore we are bound to keep all his commandments,"[13] not because we are under a covenant of works, but due to the promises of the covenant of grace. This is what Paul meant when he said, "You are not under law but under grace" (Rom. 6:14). Keeping the Ten Commandments shows the character of those renewed in God's image under grace, not placing them under law instead of grace.

Why is it vital to see the law first as a reflection of God's character rather than as a covenant of works?

## How Does the Sabbath Relate to Covenant Theology?

The Sabbath predates both the covenants of works and grace (Gen. 2:1–3). Like the tree of life, the Sabbath is also a pledge of eternal life and rest in God (Heb. 4:9–11). The Sabbath points us every week to eternal fellowship with the triune God. Through the Sabbath, God showed that he had this goal in mind for his people, whether in the covenant of works or grace. We might have expected that when God barred Adam from the tree of life, he would have taken away the Sabbath as well. Instead, God left the Sabbath as a weekly pledge of everlasting rest with God, which continues to the end of the world. While I don't have space to argue this point here, or to address the change of the day from the last to the first day of the week, treating the Sabbath as a perpetual pledge of everlasting rest until Christ's return seems to stand behind the argument of Hebrews 4:1–11.[14]

The Sabbath is a blessing under the covenant of grace. God told Israel, "Above all you shall keep my Sabbaths, for this is a sign between me and you throughout your generations, that you may know that

13  WSC q. 44 (*CCC* 420).
14  See Joseph A. Pipa, *The Lord's Day* (Fearn, UK: Christian Focus, 1997).

I, the LORD, sanctify you" (Ex. 31:13). Keeping the Sabbath "holy" means dedicating it to God's worship as we look forward to worship in heaven. Acting like the Sabbath simply teaches us not to work and to do what we find to be restful inverts the covenant of grace, making it about us, then others, then God. When God tells you to "turn back your foot from the Sabbath" (Isa. 58:13), you should think of God in the burning bush telling Moses, "Take your sandals off your feet, for the place on which you are standing is holy ground" (Ex. 3:5). We honor and delight in the Sabbath not by doing our own pleasure or "talking idly" but by taking pleasure in God's worship and talking about him (Isa. 58:13). God gave us one day in seven to devote ourselves to public, family, and private worship because the covenant of grace directs us to the blessing of eternal fellowship and rest with God in heaven.[15] The weekly Sabbath leads us steadily by the hand toward the resurrection.

In other words, we have even better grounds for delighting in the Sabbath under the new covenant because of the finished work of Christ than Adam and the old covenant saints did (Heb. 4:10). It is truly a great blessing that the Sabbath continues in every stage of the covenant of grace.

How can the Sabbath help us enjoy the promises of the covenant of grace?

### Are the Children of Believers Members of the New Covenant?

Relying on the Scripture evidence for this point in preceding chapters, the answer is yes, they are members of the new covenant. This is why they become church members through baptism. God has always

---

15 See Ryan M. McGraw, *The Day of Worship: Reassessing the Christian Life in Light of the Sabbath* (Grand Rapids, MI: Reformation Heritage Books, 2011).

brought believers and their children into the administration of the covenant, even if some don't ultimately partake of the essence of the covenant. They are heirs of the promises, not heirs of regeneration and union with Christ.

However, while they are members of the covenant by birthright, they are not members of the church until baptism. Baptism is the means of adding members to the church (e.g., Acts 2:41). Membership in the covenant of grace is the ground of administering baptism, whether to adults or to infants. In both cases, the church's task is to lead people to repentance toward God and faith in Jesus Christ (Acts 20:21), teaching them in dependence on the Spirit to live by faith in the Son of God. In every case, the time of conversion is tied not to the moment of baptism but to the Spirit's work in uniting them to Christ through faith, whether or not they know when this happened.

In what sense are children members of the new covenant?

## How Do Baptism and the Lord's Supper Differ as Covenant Signs?

Again, the chapters above answer this point already, but there are at least two things to add:

First, infant baptism does not require infant communion. There is a difference between the sign of regeneration and union with Christ, initiating the Christian life, and the sign of ongoing communion with Christ through active faith and repentance. This is why baptism happens once only, while the Lord's Supper is repeated. One sacrament requires faith, while the other presupposes it.

Second, the parallels between circumcision and baptism and the Passover and the Lord's Supper illustrate the differences in observing both sets of sacraments. While Israelite families participated in the first Passover by necessity, the annual Passover only required adult male participation, leaving the attendance of others optional at the most (e.g., Ex. 23:14, 17; Deut. 16:12–16). This is likely why Luke singled out Jesus attending the feast at twelve years old (Luke 2:42). The point is that circumcision and the Passover did not have the same necessity for covenant membership. Uncircumcised people were cut out of God's covenant (Gen. 17:14), while the Passover was less restrictive and assumed older participants. Children eventually asked their parents what the feast meant, and they grew into explicit faith, taking ownership of the covenant (Ex. 12:26). Failure to circumcise was effectively covenant breaking and excommunication, while waiting to take the Passover was not.

These parallels hold for baptism and the Lord's Supper as well. Baptism initiates church membership and urges Christian faith and life, while the Lord's Supper nourishes active faith in those of age, though we can't adequately set an appropriate age at which children publicly profess their faith in and obedience to Christ. This leaves us with the rule of baptizing believing households, while applying the need to discern the Lord's body to the Lord's Supper as described in 1 Corinthians 11.[16]

Why does infant baptism not require infant communion?

## How Does Covenant Theology Affect Assurance of Salvation?

Personal assurance of salvation involves two sides of a coin. First, we must be assured of Christ's sufficiency as mediator and of his willingness to save all who come to him. Second, we must be assured that we have both genuine faith in Christ and the Spirit in our hearts. The

16 For more detail on this question, see Cornelis P. Venema, *Children at the Lord's Table? Assessing the Case for Paedocommunion* (Grand Rapids, MI: Reformation Heritage Books, 2009).

former is largely objective, while the latter is largely subjective. Drawing from a host of Scripture passages, Westminster Larger Catechism 80 summarizes personal assurance of salvation in light of the work of the triune God in the covenant of grace:

> Such as truly believe in Christ, and endeavor to walk in all good conscience before him, may, without extraordinary revelation, by faith grounded upon the truth of God's promises, and by the Spirit enabling them to discern in themselves those graces to which the promises of life are made, and bearing witness with their spirits that they are the children of God, be infallibly assured that they are in the estate of grace, and shall persevere therein unto salvation.[17]

The next question adds that true believers may fluctuate in subjective assurance of salvation, though they are never without the Spirit, who "keeps them from sinking into utter despair."[18] Covenant theology presses the objective realities of God's actions in the covenant of grace, which need always take priority over subjective experiences of assurance. We can and will persevere to final salvation at the resurrection because the Spirit of Christ preserves us (Rom. 8:11–39).

Taking a practical example, if we lack assurance because we doubt the level of our repentance, because of indwelling sin, or because we have seen so many seemingly sincere people fall away from Christ, then it is more important to ask what we believe than what we feel. Feelings are not the object of faith; Christ is. Covenant promises, conveyed in the word and in covenant signs like baptism, teach us to expect everything from Christ, including repentance, obedience,

17  WLC q. 80 (*CCC* 360).
18  WLC q. 81 (*CCC* 361).

perseverance, and everything else we need for life and godliness. If we start thinking we only need to fix whatever hinders our assurance first before having assurance, then we will spiral downward, not exercising faith in Christ to receive what we need because we are unsure whether we have faith in Christ. The real questions are: Have you died to sin, and are you alive in Christ? Do you believe that the darkness is passing away and the true light is already shining? Do you trust the Spirit to lead you from one degree of glory to another as you behold God's glory in the face of Christ?

We should also not neglect the role of the means of grace in the church in promoting assurance of salvation. Sacraments and church membership are not grounds or substitutes for salvation in Christ, but covenant promises and signs are vehicles to draw us to the Father, through the Son, by the Spirit. While we should never replace Christ with the church or the sacraments, we should expect to meet Christ under the means of grace and in fellowship with the church.

How and why is Christ the ground of our assurance of salvation?

## How Should Covenant Theology Affect Preaching?

Covenant theology always provides the right context for preaching, reminding preachers of their goals. The covenant of grace focuses on Christ, requires faith and repentance in dependence on the Spirit, warns against falling away, and gives us everything we need to persevere through hardships. Rooting our salvation in the Savior, the covenant of redemption places our hope in Christ, the only mediator between God and man. God's covenants teach us to look forward to Christ's return and to being made like him in heaven. Appealing to the broken covenant of works shows us simultaneously our need for Christ and what Christ had to do to save us. Covenant theology either reminds us of the relationship that we have with the triune God or calls us into a proper relationship with him. In this sense, covenant theology matches the purposes of Scripture that Paul outlines in 2 Timothy 3:15–17, setting the tone for biblical preaching.

Three cautions are in order here, however. First, do not assume that your hearers understand what *covenant* means. It is easy to assume too much in preaching with the result that our hearers either do not understand our meaning, or they never define clearly what common terms mean. Have a short, easy-to-understand definition of *covenant* handy to keep hearers on track when necessary.

Second, not everything is about covenant theology. The divine attributes and Trinity come to mind, for example, which precede covenants and require explanation in their own rights. Even here, however, we apply God's attributes, names, and triunity only in the context of the covenant of grace.

Third, let the covenant shape the tone of your preaching, even if you do not always use the term *covenant*. Our preaching would be far better, with far more of the Spirit's power, if we always sought to explain Scripture, point people to Christ, tell them what God requires of them, and show how all these things lead them to the "beatific vision" in heaven. The early and medieval church did these things by teaching that these were four "senses" of Scripture (quadriga). Instead of teaching four different uses or applications of the text, this view taught that every text had four different meanings. Grounded in the literal sense of the passage, such authors treated allegory as pointing to Christ, a "tropological" sense as telling the church what to do, and an "anagogical" sense as directing people to the life to come as exegetically embedded in every text. Without abandoning the single sense of Scripture, applying our preaching in these four ways reflects the tone of the covenant of grace well. Retaining these four things as goals in preaching, instead of multiple senses of Scripture, would certainly bring great blessings to God's covenant people. Covenant theology should lead us to explain the text, to preach Christ, to move the church to action, and to direct believers to seeing God at the resurrection.

# Recommended Resources

IN ADDITION TO the resources cited in the footnotes in this book, there are a few good starting places to study covenant theology further. Books on the covenant are legion, but the following list includes some of the best, in my view. This list is intentionally short.

As far as recent books, two stand out for their depth, clarity, and simplicity:

The first is Stephen G. Myers, *God to Us: Covenant Theology in Scripture* (Grand Rapids, MI: Reformation Heritage Books, 2021). Myers argues exegetically, practically, and thoroughly for the kind of covenant theology reflected in this book. Myers' work is full and satisfying.

The other book is Richard P. Belcher, *The Fulfillment of the Promises of God: An Explanation of Covenant Theology* (Fearn, UK: Mentor, 2020). Equally clear, this book divides the material into telling the biblical narrative of covenant theology and addressing contemporary questions and problems related to the subject. Both books present what I view as a standard historic Reformed covenant theology, which has become rare in recent years.

A larger book I recommend is *Covenant Theology: Biblical, Theological, and Historical Perspectives*, ed. Guy Prentiss Waters, Nicholas J. Reid, and John R. Muether (Wheaton, IL: Crossway, 2020).

This multicontributor volume includes much useful material as well, especially in relation to church history and contemporary issues. For example, the chapters on ancient Near Eastern covenant forms, New Testament biblical studies, and new covenant theologies stand out among others. The historical and contemporary material is some of the best modern material on the covenant that I have found.

Moving to older books, I recommend Herman Witsius, *The Economy of the Covenants between God and Man*, ed. Joel R. Beeke, trans. William Crookshank, 2 vols. (Grand Rapids, MI: Reformation Heritage Books, 2010). This is a noted classic, for good reasons. Despite the misleading English subtitle, this is not a system or body of divinity but merely a treatment of the covenants. It was not a biblically grounded alternative to systematic theology, as many have assumed. Witsius's work is packed with Scripture and filled with excellent contrasts and summary statements, and he devoted distinct chapters to topics like circumcision not found as clearly in other works. The amount of Scripture he uses may overwhelm some readers, yet this will be exactly what others are looking for.

Patrick Gillespie's two volumes on covenant theology are some of the best treatments of the subject: *The Ark of the Testament Opened* [. . .] (London: R. C.,1661) and *The Ark of the Covenant Opened* [. . .] (London: Tho. Parkhurst, 1667). The first book unfolds the covenants of works and grace, while the latter expounds the covenant of redemption. No one is better at understanding the relationship and distinction between the covenants of redemption and grace. His definitions of covenants and categorizations of different kinds of covenants, as well as his attention to the covenant of works, are merely some reasons why these two books are so useful. Unfortunately, neither book is currently in print, but they are readily available electronically through Post-Reformation Digital Library (https://www.prdl.org).

Francis Turretin's *Institutes of Elenctic Theology*, 3 vols., ed. James T. Dennison, trans. George Musgrave Giger (Phillipsburg, NJ: P&R, 1992–1997), is solid and well-balanced on covenant topics, which readers can find easily in his table of contents. While Turretin's scholastic style will be foreign, if not challenging, to many modern readers, he never left anyone taking the time to read him without giving them exceptionally clear distinctions and arguments on any topic. His covenant theology is well-rounded and outstanding.

John Calvin's *Institutes of the Christian Religion*, ed. John T. McNeill, trans. Ford Lewis Battles (Philadelphia: Westminster, 1960), is also useful, especially given that he dedicates much time to covenant theology in relation to the sacraments. Calvin overstresses the continuity of the old and new covenants at points, leaving one wondering whether the Spirit's work differed between the old and new covenants. Yet few authors make the breathtaking unity of the covenant of grace come to life like Calvin.

Though not strictly a covenant theology, Augustine's *City of God*, trans. Henry Bettenson, (London: Penguin, 1984), contains much profound material about the unity of the church in the Old and New Testaments. Very few books have never gone out of print, and *City of God* is one of them. This is particularly noteworthy when we keep in mind that the church distributed the book through handmade copies for a thousand years before the invention of the printing press.

# General Index

Abraham, 4, 26–27, 31, 32, 34–38, 43, 44, 45, 59, 60, 71, 76, 86, 88, 89, 94
  blessing of, 4, 34, 43, 45, 88
  seed of, 27, 36, 44, 71
Abrahamic covenant, 4, 27, 36, 37, 38
abusing the elements (Communion), 65
Adam, 18–19, 20–21, 22, 23, 31, 32, 33, 35, 38, 40, 44, 58, 59, 74, 75, 82, 86, 97, 98, 114–16, 117, 118, 119
amillennialism, 102
antinomian, 2
antinomianism, 104, 105
Apocrypha, apocryphal books, 107–10
apostasy, 15, 112–13
Aquinas. *See* Thomas Aquinas
*Ark of the Covenant Opened, The* (Gillespie), 128–29
*Ark of the Testament Opened, The* (Gillespie), 128–29
Augustine of Hippo, 98, 107–8, 109, 129

baptism
  children and, 88. *See also* infant baptism
  correct mode of, 66
  as a covenant sign

  how it differs from the Lord's Supper, 120–21
  how it helps us know the triune God's glory, 65–70
  the demands of, 69
  and faith, 67
  household, 36–37, 53, 86, 88, 121
  as a sacrament, what is revealed by, 66
  what it shows us about salvation, 68
beatific vision, 101, 102, 124
Bel and the Dragon, 107
Bible
  how covenants unify the themes of the Bible, 14–15
  three categories of people presented in the, 112
  two ways covenant theology teaches us to joyfully read the, 58–60
  why Protestants do not include the apocryphal books in the, 107–10
  *See also* Scripture
blessing
  of Abraham, 4, 34, 43, 45, 88
  why covenant theology is a, 4–8
books
  apocryphal, 71n5
  on the importance of the Trinity in Christian life and practice (by McGraw), 71n5

# Scripture Index

SCRIPTURE INDEX